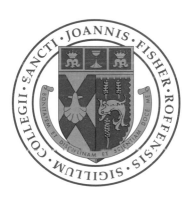

Hard Work

Remaking the American Labor Movement

Rick Fantasia
Kim Voss

UNIVERSITY OF CALIFORNIA PRESS

Berkeley   Los Angeles   London

University of California Press
Berkeley and Los Angeles, California

University of California Press, Ltd.
London, England

Library of Congress Cataloging-in-Publication Data

Fantasia, Rick.
    [Des syndicats domestiquâes. English]
    Hard work : remaking the American labor movement /
Rick Fantasia, Kim Voss.
        p.   cm.
Revised and enlarged edition of Des syndicats domestiquâes,
which was originally written in English, then translated into
French and published in Paris by Raisons d'Agir, 2003.
    Includes bibliographical references and index.
    ISBN 0–520–24013–8 (cloth : alk. paper)—
ISBN 0–520–24090–1 (pbk. : alk. paper)
        1. Labor movement—United States.   2. Labor unions—
Social aspects—United States.   3. Labor unions—United
States—Management.   4. Industrial relations—United
States.   5. Bureaucracy—United States.   I. Voss, Kim.
II. Title.
HD6508.F23513   2004
331.88'0973—dc22   2003022988

Manufactured in the United States of America
13   12   11   10   09   08   07   06   05   04
10   9   8   7   6   5   4   3   2   1

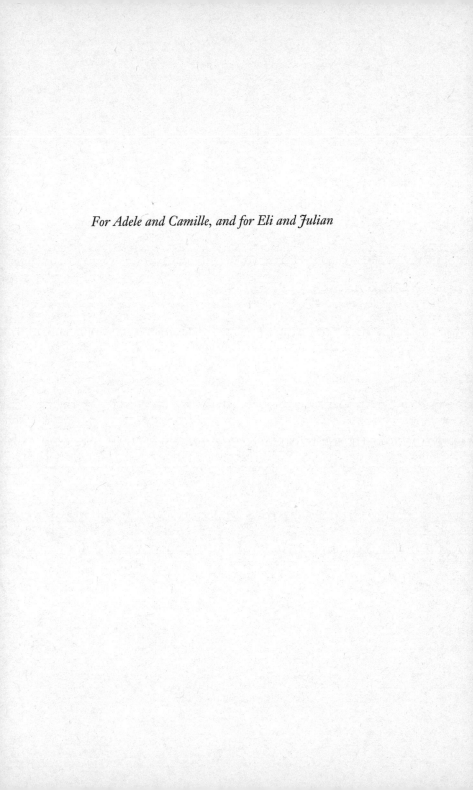

For Adele and Camille, and for Eli and Julian

CONTENTS

ILLUSTRATIONS

FIGURES

TABLE

PREFACE

"A bit unusual and a little special"

To readers of American academic books this volume will seem unusual: it is too short to carry a substantial body of new data and its rhetorical stance is too engaged to pretend an objective pose. Moreover, it reads like a work written for an intelligent reader who is somewhat uninformed about how labor works in the United States. If all of this makes for a strange book, it is probably because it bears certain traces of its origin as a work written for the European, specifically the French, reader.

Although we penned (or rather, keystroked) this book in our native English, we initially did so for a unique French publisher, Raisons D'Agir Editions, an imprint of a series founded by the French sociologist Pierre Bourdieu and his associates in the wake of the massive strikes and social mobilizations that engulfed France in December 1995. The idea for our project took root in late 1997, when, at the urging of Loic Wacquant, Fantasia wrote to Bourdieu with a proposal for an article for one of Bourdieu's journals. Fantasia proposed writing about the reform underway in the U.S. labor movement and its significance for U.S. society and the world. Professor Bourdieu published the letter as an essay in his journal, *LIBER, Revue Européen des Livres*, and requested a book on the topic for the Raisons D'Agir series. Fantasia, who is familiar with French culture and politics, recognized the significance of the opportunity and accepted the invitation without hesitation.

The celebrated editor Andrè Schiffrin has called Raisons D'Agir (which means "Reasons to Act") an "inspiring example" for producing books that have "dominated French best-seller lists with their new ideas, polemics, and criticism," and that have served as a shining exception to the rule of market dominion in the world of publishing.[1] Produced under the direction of Bourdieu, the small, inexpensive books are recognized as politically provocative and analytically rigorous intellectual interventions in the vigorous public debate in France over the social costs of neoliberal reform.

Some months later both of us, Fantasia and Voss, met for a long lunch at an ASA meeting in San Francisco where we discussed the trajectory and dynamics of the U.S. labor movement. We recognized an intellectual and political compatibility, and our discussions soon made it apparent that it would be both beneficial and completely natural to make the Raisons D'Agir book project a joint and equal one. Voss was enthusiastic about the book because it provided an opportunity to write for a European audience and because it seemed the perfect occasion to explain the U.S. labor movement to *American* colleagues, students, and activists, many of whom know a great deal about most contemporary social movements but surprisingly little about unions or workers' collective actions. Thus began a collaboration that has been a complete joy. Of course, in the process, we worked through our intellectual disagreements as well as the inevitable frustrations caused by the difficulty of synchronizing writing schedules and coordinating work calendars in the midst of two overly busy lives lived on opposite ends of the continent. In the end, we have produced a very different book than we initially envisioned, one that is better than either of us could have made alone.

Although our book was next in the queue for publication in the Raisons D'Agir series, Bourdieu demonstrated great patience and understanding with the delays in submitting it. We knew nothing of his illness and, as it happened, our manuscript finally arrived on his desk less than two weeks before he passed away in late January 2002. We were deeply saddened by his passing, but gratified to learn that Bourdieu had expressed his contentment upon receiving our manuscript, which had been judged "excellent" by one of his close associates.

We always knew that our book should appear in English and sought a publisher in the United States while working on the French edition. We were very fortunate that Naomi Schneider and the University of California Press, both at the top of our wish lists for editor and English-language publisher, took on our project. We thank them for their accommodation and support of our somewhat unusual book.

This UC Press version is somewhat longer than the French, but otherwise retains most of the features of the Raisons D'Agir edition. Among other things, we have taken certain polemical license that is perhaps less common on this side of the Atlantic.

We have also generally avoided the kind of rhetorical stance that academics normally take when writing for those within their own disciplinary specialty. For example, we cite the work of others for support, but we have not engaged in the ritual of gratuitous citation that is a convention of academic writing (including some of our own). Rather, we have sought to accomplish a certain synthesis of both our own work and the work of others, so that the nonspecialist will not feel excluded. Moreover, we do not try to adjudicate between various points of view about American labor and the labor movement. We know the different points of view, for we have read and digested them and have spent a good portion of our adult lives considering them. Instead, we intended this to be a book about what *we* think about labor and what we think others ought to know about it, and for better or worse, that is pretty much what this work is.

Certain analytical features may also make the book seem unusual. These have been informed by the radically relational method of analysis developed by Pierre Bourdieu, whose sociological approach is deliberately counterintuitive. Among other things, it encouraged us to depart from the confines of "productivism" as we considered the situation of labor in the United States, so that consumption and production could be considered together as mutually constituting practices and as dual mechanisms of exploitation, rather than as distinct spheres of economic activity. In the same way, the reader may notice a tendency to draw symbolic and material effects of social processes together, rather than treating them as dichotomous or distinctive, thereby elevating symbolic representation to coequal analytical status with the materiality of social life. However imperfectly we have employed Bourdieu's analytical lens, we believe his intellectual influence contributes to making this book a little special. Ultimately, our goal was to clearly—and without euphemism—uncover the social logic of American labor.

Special thanks are due Carl Somers, who provided invaluable research assistance for Chapters 3 and 4, and to Steve Lopez, Teresa Sharpe, and two anonymous reviewers at UC Press for their critical comments on the manuscript as a whole. Thanks to the no-name labor study group from Amherst, Massachusetts (Mark Brenner, Dan Clawson, Harris Freeman, Tom Juravich, Stephanie Luce, Dale Melcher, and Eve Weinbaum, for their comments on and criticisms of Chapter 3), and to the audience at the Berkeley Sociology Colloquium who asked probing questions about the ideas presented in Chapter 4. More thanks go to Loic Wacquant for helping to facilitate this project from the very beginning, to Andy Levin for his help early on, to Larry Mishel and Mike Hout for providing statistics and advice for Figure 1.1, to Rick Jaffe for his help and support throughout, and to Jerome Bourdieu, Pascale Casanova, and Franck Poupeau for their work on the French edition. The Institute of Industrial Relations and the Committee on Research at the University of California, Berkeley, and Smith College provided financial support for the research and writing.

CHAPTER ONE

Why Labor Matters

The Underside of the "American Model"

In the American popular imagination and in the mainstream press, the United States is presented as being superior to Western Europe in almost every way. Newspaper articles boast that the American economy is a miraculous jobs machine and disparage the high unemployment rates in Europe; they emphasize high productivity growth and scorn "Eurosclerosis."[1] They tout the unprecedented levels of economic creativity unleashed by the "new economy" of the 1990s and criticize Europeans for clinging to outmoded ways of life. In addition, Americans believe, and are repeatedly told, that they enjoy the highest standard of living and have more job opportunities than any other country (in addition to being the most free people on earth and living in the most democratic of all societies).

Especially in the booming 1990s, American leaders and economic experts used this supposed superiority to proclaim American neoliberalism as a model that the rest of the world should follow. From the elegant meeting halls of the G7, to corporate boardrooms, to ambassadorial suites, European countries were told that they could not hope to compete in the new global economy unless they admitted the error of their ways, scaled back their antiquated welfare states, and became—like the United States—more fiscally responsible, more friendly to business and entrepreneurship, and more flexible. Poorer countries throughout the world were lectured even more relentlessly, while being mercilessly squeezed by the "structural adjustment" policies of the U.S.-led International Monetary Fund.

Despite the recent troubles of the U.S. economy, the conviction that U.S.-style neoliberalism remains the best economic model, both here and abroad, goes virtually unquestioned. We are told repeatedly that America's current economic and social woes will be solved by more of the same policies that purportedly generated the boom in the first place: more deregulation, further privatization, and greater tax cuts (especially for the wealthiest Americans).

We contend that perceptions of U.S. superiority, even during the boom years, have been largely an optical illusion, and that the American model is not all that it is cracked up to be. In fact, the "new economy" is not very different from the old and U.S. job creation has not been particularly noteworthy or distinct from that in many European countries.

What *is* truly distinctive about the United States when compared to Western Europe is a lack of social provisions—such as national health insurance, universal child care, and paid parental leave—as well as scandalously high levels of poverty and inequality. In fact, most working-class Europeans have a better standard of living than most working-class Americans.[2]

European families are often better off than their American

counterparts in large part because a historical weakness and a narrowness of vision have prevented American labor from effectively challenging the power of U.S. capital within the American political and economic system. This weakness undergirds the emergence of neoliberalism as the dominant political discourse today in the United States and allows U.S. capital to attempt to impose the American model on the rest of the world.

But the U.S. labor movement is not static. Today it is undergoing a fitful reinvention, to emerge out of its weakest point in fifty years. The movement is now positioning itself to organize and mobilize against the neoliberal present, to become what it never has been before—a genuine counterweight to the power of U.S. capital. The struggle is crucial and gave us good reason to write this book. Our goal is to train the reader's ear to interpret the sound of labor in U.S. society, for the changes being attempted within the labor movement can be fairly considered to be among the most important social developments that U.S. society has seen in decades. As weak and unfit as they are, American unions are nevertheless the most important potential social defense against a dystopian future.

THE HEART OF DARKNESS AT THE CENTER OF THE "NEW" ECONOMY

In the United States the business press, along with a veritable army of journalists, academics, and politicians who are in thrall to business, have long been involved in the painstaking work of projecting an image of capitalism as much larger than itself, as something transcendent. Nowhere has this been more evident than with regard to what is variously called "high technology," the "information economy," and "e-commerce," terms designating the broad application of computer technologies to business activities. This sector, which even before its recent decline was a less materially significant part of the U.S. economy than the promotional hyperbole ever allowed, has been portrayed as a world comprised of "smart workers" (rather than mindless drones), of "clean production" (rather than dirty, smoke-belching factories), and as a genuine meritocracy (clever entrepreneurial inventiveness is valued above inherited wealth or social standing).[3] The "new economy" is thus often presented as an Elysian field of economic creativity in which the felt unpleasantness of actual economic activity and its accompanying negative social effects have somehow been overcome. Totally obscured in this presentation is the pervasiveness of cheap and insecure labor.

The one thing the so-called New Economy has seemed able to produce most abundantly has been tales about its own invincibility, tales that are reinforced by the endless stories of young internet entrepreneurs suddenly finding themselves awash in unimaginable riches. Such narratives have become a standard part of a literature of envy that continues to feed a seemingly endless fascination with the personal net worth of those who are, almost literally, capable of purchasing the planet. With breathless reverence, journalists for newspapers and magazines, both on- and off-line, have manufactured heroic tales of the business lives of billionaires (Bill Gates of Microsoft, Steve Case of America Online, and Jeffrey Bezos of Amazon.com, most notably), who are portrayed as the personification of youthfulness, entrepreneurialism, and studied informality that are said to typify the "new economy." Like most mythic constructions, this one has required that the means of its fabrication remain obscure; thus, the model has depended on the belief in an economy that somehow could float above the mundane exigencies of labor, of time, and of social inequality. Although the high-technology sector has spawned a rich vocabulary of euphemisms to conceal it, the exploitation of nonunion labor remains at its very core.

Prior to the wave of recession that rolled through the areas of high-technology concentration, namely, the "Silicon Valley" of northern California and Seattle in the Pacific Northwest, the meteoric rise in the number of "paper millionaires" (employees holding stock options worth more than 1 million dollars) seemed an impressive achievement. However, even during the boom, most employees in the high-technology sector were neither entrepreneurs, nor managers, nor even highly paid software developers. So although the extravagant wealth of the top executives attracted much of the attention, the success of many "e-companies" like Amazon.com (the Seattle-based book-order company) has actually rested on a labor-intensive distribution system that depends on thousands of low-wage-earning, often temporary workers. For a mere 7 dollars an hour, these workers hurriedly pack books into boxes for shipping; meanwhile, hundreds of harried service representatives spend their days in tiny cubicles responding to customer e-mail. They also earn less than a living wage.[4]

This is a world where the janitors who clean the buildings that house Cisco Systems, Sun Microsystems, and the other pillars of the "new economy" can barely afford to pay to house themselves, because they are so poorly paid by the subcontracting firms who employ them (in a situation that relieves the high-tech giants of any responsibility). Often three and four families have been forced to share a single dwelling in a geographic area where it is even a struggle for an immigrant worker to be able to afford the monthly rent required to live in something as modest as a converted garage. In the Silicon Valley area the proliferation of millionaires has pushed real estate prices so high that garages, pool houses, and other spaces that are generally considered uninhabitable elsewhere in the country routinely double as rental properties. And every year some 20–30,000 people reportedly find themselves homeless in the Silicon Valley.[5]

Although they are an important part of the industry's reality, high-income software engineers and computer programmers, who work at firms like Microsoft and earn hefty salaries plus stock options, were never the entire picture. Working right next to them, during the boom as well as today, are so-called temporary employees who also log seventy-hour workweeks, but under very different terms.[6] Frequently employed for extended periods, but hired through and paid by temporary-employment agencies, these "temps" are offered little job security, no stock options, and no pension plan.[7] To ensure that the number of highly paid "regulars" were limited, the technology industry successfully pressured Congress to pass legislation to loosen the high-technology labor market by doubling the number of visas for educated foreigners who take temporary, specialized jobs in the U.S. computer industry. At the height of the dot.com boom, technology firms contributed tens of millions of dollars to federal election campaigns in a successful effort to pressure Congress to raise to 195,000 the number of temporary H1-B work visas granted annually (a substantial increase from the previous level of 115,000 annual visas set in 1998, which had already doubled from the 65,000 limit the year before). Recently, yet another visa program has been exploited to increase the number of "temporary" workers. High-tech consultancy firms use the L-1 visa program to transport foreign workers to the United States so that they can then hire them out as "consultants" to other companies.

These laws amount to a high-technology "bracero" program under which immigrant workers enter the country on temporary work visas and are then prohibited from switching employers. Despite token provisions meant to allay the concerns of trade unions, it is expected that the effect of these laws is to depress wages and to further impede the growth of unionization in an industry that until now has been virtually union-free.[8] In addition to being able to hire and fire, employers now have the power to affect the immigration status of their workers, because the law permits them to facilitate the deportation of any worker on a temporary visa who might seek to organize a union, who might file discrimination charges, or who might simply refuse to work overtime.

With contingency as its leitmotif, the "new economy" has come to represent something of a "model within the model," an economic sector largely able to establish its own rules without having to defer to "past practices," to overcome union bargaining structures, or to dismantle the prophylactic mechanisms of state regulation (deregulation representing an act of state as surely as taxation or war making). Within this sector contingency has been elevated to a virtue, and no one has paid much attention to the extent to which the dot.com boom was built on a foundation of low wages and transitory jobs. During the booming 1990s while the average yearly compensation of Silicon Valley's highest paid executives nearly quadrupled to more than 7 million dollars a year (not counting stock options), the wages of the bottom quarter of workers dropped 20 percent, to just slightly more than

9 dollars an hour, far below the 14 dollars an hour that constituted a living wage for a family of one adult and two children. When some such low-wage workers at Amazon.com began to talk about organizing a union, however, the managers of the new economy revealed just how similar they were in their thinking to the managers of the old economy—they hired union-busting consultants and fought tooth and nail to keep their enterprise union-free.[9]

THE "SOCIAL LIFE"
OF THE AMERICAN WORKER

The neoliberal onslaught has been so complete in the United States because the forces promoting it have not had to face the kind of institutional and political obstacles encountered elsewhere. The combination of an institutionally precarious labor movement and inconspicuous left-wing or progressive politics have produced a truly "exceptional" industrialized society in the United States in contrast to Western Europe. This concrete historical circumstance has also made it an object of emulation, a model. In other words, much of what has made the United States exceptional can be boiled down to the diminished presence of labor at an institutional level. This, in turn, has made it appear reasonable to exclude labor symbolically, thus producing the kind of sanitized version of the reality of the American model that is represented to the rest of the world. We explore how this came about and explain the social mechanisms that sustain it and the social forces struggling to change it. Effectively, the purpose of neoliberal social policy in the United States has been to erode public services and collective structures. Individual actors displace "society" symbolically, while the sources of public power are dismantled institutionally.[10] Presented as a noble cultural trait and celebrated as prideful self-reliance, individualism has had a relentless and overarching ideological presence in the life of American society, maintained and reproduced in a multitude of practices, both formal and informal, that foster separateness and discourage social solidarity. Indeed, individualism can be considered one of four interconnected and mutually reinforcing elements (along with deregulation, decentralization, and privatization) that characterize the neoliberal program of social reform. It is important to recognize individualism not as a simple cultural trait, but as one component of a set of practices that is simultaneously institutional and mental, and whose effect is to leave real individuals, real citizens, entirely defenseless against the corporate power unleashed by the three other elements.

Of course, in the felt experience of most Americans, individualism is not necessarily perceived as a *lack* of anything, either of collective efficacies, of social solidarity, or of public aid. In a society that has largely abdicated collective responsibility, one simply "makes do" with whatever resources are at hand, while what is at hand for any individual is therefore heavily dependent on one's immediate social circumstances and resources. For example, the relatively weak institutional ties that prevail between the state and the economy in the United States, relative to Europe, means that finding a job, particularly for those with few qualifications, depends heavily on information acquired informally, through private friendship and kinship networks, rather than in the context of a more institutionalized system of job tracks that serve as channels between school and employment and that facilitate a relatively fluid transition between the two. In the United States the dependence on informal and localized social networks represents a practice that has the effect of reproducing the existing social (and hierarchic) distribution of labor markets, of creating racial and ethnic concentrations in workplaces, and of converting even the smallest accumulation of social capital into a potentially crucial economic resource ("it's not what you know, it's who you know," as the popular aphorism holds).[11]

American workers must navigate a labor market that is composed of highly decentralized workplaces and where job skills tend to be acquired relatively informally, and unsystematically. In Europe formal training programs provide occupational qualifications that are transferable to other job sites; in the United States workers tend to learn "on the job," acquiring firm-specific skills on an informal and individual basis.[12] Similarly, in contrast to Europe, where wage setting is centralized and coordinated, in the United States pay scales are set for a largely nonunion workforce through the mostly decentralized and uncoordinated "interactions of tens of thousands of firms and millions of workers in the labor market."[13] Although large firms and unionized companies do maintain formal pay schedules and rely on systematic methods to determine industry standards, the lack of overall coordination results in much wider wage disparities among workers doing the same job in different locations than is the case in European countries.[14]

The prime selling point of the American model is the claim that the United States has done rather well, relative to Europe, in creating jobs over the past several decades. But certain qualifications must immediately be added to this assertion. The first is a temporal one. If we consider only the 1975–85 time frame, a period when most of Western Europe was experiencing slow economic growth and rising rates of unemployment and the United States was creating some twenty million jobs, we would be left with the impression that the United States was truly an impressive "jobs machine." A shift to the 1989–95 time frame, however, indicates that the U.S. rate of employment growth slowed to 1.0 percent, a rate that differed only a little from the 0.9 percent average of other rich, industrialized nations. And if we move to the 1995–2000 period, we find that the U.S. rate of 1.6 percent employment growth was exceeded in eight countries: Ireland (5.5 percent), Spain (3.7 percent), the Netherlands (2.7 percent), Canada (2.2 percent), Finland (2.2 percent), Portugal (2.2 percent), Australia (1.9 percent), and Norway (1.9 percent).[15]

Furthermore, a high proportion of the jobs that have been created in the United States are contingent, or nonstandard jobs (part-time, temporary, on-call, subcontracted, self-employed). These are routinely less secure, less well-paid, and offer few benefits such as paid medical or dental insurance, paid vacations, and training. Wage declines in the early 1980s drove large numbers of American workers to seek second and third jobs, so that by 1999, 5.9 percent of the workforce (amounting to eight million workers) held two or more jobs, many of them part-time and concentrated in low-paying industries and occupations. Multiple job holdings will likely increase since of the dozen occupations that are projected to produce the most jobs by the year 2008, half currently pay wages at or below the official poverty level.[16]

Fueling the expansion of the part-time labor force has been the rapid growth of chain establishments in the service sector, the most successful of which are built on a foundation of high sales volume, high technology, and low labor costs. The management of these firms require high levels of labor "flexibility" that is much easier to achieve with a part-time, nonunion labor force. As one manager admitted to a researcher, "The pluses of hiring part-time people are the [low] rate of pay that you're able to pay them, the increased [schedule] flexibility that it will allow you, particularly if you have a varying business, varying volume."[17] Fast-food companies like McDonald's maintain a workforce with up to 80 percent part-time employees, and some retail chains hide the size of their part-time labor force by simply redefining the terms. According to Naomi Klein, Wal-Mart is able to claim that 70 percent of its labor force works full time by defining "full time" as twenty-eight hours per week.[18] The Starbucks chain of coffee shops counts 57 percent of its workers as full time, but defines "full time" as twenty hours per week, and The Gap clothing store deems 70 percent of its employees "full time" by labeling thirty hours per week as full-time employment.[19] When we add to this the fact that the "temporary-help" industry in the United States grew from .4 million workers in 1982 to 3.0 million in 1999, we approach a situation in which *one out of four* U.S. workers is employed in some form of nonstandard job arrangement, a situation that some have clearly chosen voluntarily, but that many others have not.[20]

Just as claims about job creation in the United States must be treated with a measure of skepticism, the same holds for claims about the unemployment level. Although it is true that the overall unemployment rate has tended to be impressively low in the United States for the past two decades, that is not so very exceptional, for it has actually been even lower in a number of other OECD countries. While the 2001 U.S. unemployment rate of 4.8 percent is indeed less than the 6.9 percent average of all OECD countries, six European countries had unemployment rates in 2001 that were below the U.S. rate: the Netherlands (2.4 percent), Switzerland (2.5 percent), Austria (3.6 percent), Norway (3.6 percent), Portugal (4.1 percent), and Denmark (4.3 percent). A handful of countries also had lower unemployment rates in 1989, and in 1979 the U.S. unemployment rate of 5.8 percent *exceeded* the OECD average rate of 4.4 percent.[21] Furthermore, it is estimated that the millions of poor males, predominantly racial and ethnic minorities caught up in the U.S. penal system, have contributed to a full 2 percent artificial reduction in the unemployment rate throughout the 1990s.[22] This would seem to be an especially significant point if we consider the admittedly counterintuitive idea that youth incarceration in the United States essentially represents a perverse, though largely unintended "solution" to the problem of youth unemployment. When *adult* unemployment rates are considered apart from those of youth, those rates appear to have been similar or slightly *lower* in major European countries than in the United States in recent years.[23] Additionally, in its monthly household survey from which the U.S. unemployment rate is actually derived, the U.S. Census Bureau counts anyone over the age of sixteen who has worked *just one hour in the previous week* as "in the labor force and working," a standard that would seem to represent a rather uncertain foundation for an edifice as grand as the "Great American Jobs Machine." Besides, unlike in Europe, no matter how substantial a job is in the United States, unless it is unionized its occupant can always be discharged by an employer at a moment's notice, without reason or warning and without severance compensation (with the exception of certain categories of schoolteachers, university professors, and civil servants with tenure, as well as senior executives in possession of a severance contract). Overall then, it is clear that despite several decades of rhetoric and a host of questionable assumptions, when the rates of employment and unemployment are viewed in the social context in which labor is actually performed in the United States, the situation does not appear nearly as distinctive or as exceptional as it has been made out to be.

With regard to the wages associated with these jobs, the average weekly earnings of those 80 percent of Americans who are production and nonsupervisory workers fell by 16 percent between the years 1973 and 1995 (adjusted for inflation).[24] Significant wage growth did occur during the boom years between 1995–2000 (1.9 percent per year), but this must be viewed against the backdrop of a much lengthier, steadier, and more substantial wage *decline* that transpired for more than two decades among male "blue collar," "service," and many categories of "white-collar" workers in the United States.[25] This was a period in which the share of workers earning poverty-level wages rose among most groups, and although the share fell between 1995 and 2000, roughly *one-quarter* of the workforce still brings home only poverty-level wages.[26] Overall, that portion of the American workforce with less than a high school education earned $2.16 per hour *less* in 2001 than they earned in 1973, and those workers with a high school diploma earned $0.55 *less* per hour in 2001 than they did in 1973 (together these categories constituted a full 42 percent of all workers in 2001).[27] Workers with college degrees enjoyed real wage growth but they made up only about one-quarter of the workforce. While the education/wage differential is often portrayed in the media as a higher education "premium" that accrues to those who have successfully attained a university education (often implicitly posed as a shortcoming of those who have not) the data indicate that the primary reason for an increased wage gap between university-educated and other workers is less the strong growth of the university wage, and more the sharp decline of wages among non-university-educated workers.[28]

Meanwhile, at the other end of the social cosmos the pay of corporate CEOs has soared since the 1980s, with top corporate leaders now collecting more than 11 million dollars in compensation annually, and the average CEO receiving 245 times the pay of the average production worker.[29] This ratio is up sharply from what it was in 1980 when the ratio of CEO pay to average worker pay was 42 to 1, and it is much higher than it is in European and other advanced countries, where CEOs earn on average only 28 percent of what their American counterparts make. Figure 1.1 shows the growing distance between worker pay and CEO pay in the United States, demonstrating how even during the expansionary period 1995–2000, workers' real wages lagged behind productivity as well as behind CEO compensation. Once upon a time, when unions were stronger, workers reaped some of the benefits of productivity gains, but beginning in the 1980s, the rewards of productivity increases went overwhelming to CEOs and the largest investors rather than to workers.[30]

Wealth represents an even more significant form of inequality than annual income, and in the United States, the richest 5 percent of the population owns 59 percent of the wealth, more than the remaining 95 percent combined. Today there is greater wealth concentration in the United States than in any other advanced democratic country. It is worth noting that this has only become the case over the last twenty-five or thirty years. Until the early 1970s, the United States had *lower* wealth inequality

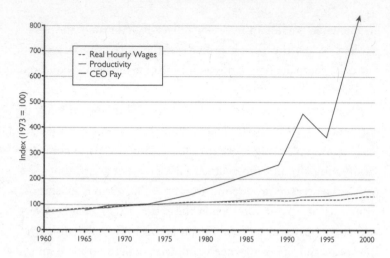

Figure 1.1. *The Growing Divergence Between CEO and Average Worker Pay.* Sources: Productivity and wage data are from the Department of Labor, Bureau of Labor Statistics. The data measure output per hour and hourly compensation in the nonfarm business sector, 1960–2001 (www.bls.gov). To get real hourly compensation, the Bureau of Labor Statistics figures were deflated by the Economic Policy Institute (EPI), using the CPI-U-RS series. CEO pay was also provided by the EPI and is based on *Wall Street Journal* and Mercer surveys. In general, EPI reports lower figures for the ratio of CEO to average worker pay than do other sources such as *Business Week.* Thus the divergence between CEO and worker pay depicted in Figure 1.1 should be considered a conservative estimate.

than most European nations. However one cuts this cake, the level of inequality in the United States is extraordinary and growing dramatically, but equally remarkable is that most Americans appear to be completely accommodated to it.[31]

For most workers in the United States there has not only been a decline in real wages over the past three decades, but also a decline in what Americans call "fringe benefits," a term that has come to accurately reflect the institutional status of social provision in American society. In the absence of a universal health insurance system and in the context of a mostly private system of medical care, the employer provision of health insurance is a virtual necessity for most workers in the United States, but between 1979 and 2000 the share of workers covered by employer-provided health insurance in the private sector dropped from 70.2 to 63.4 percent, a reduction of 6.8 percent, while employer-provided retirement pensions also declined, leaving in 2000 only 49.6 percent of the private-sector workforce with the ability to depend on one.[32] Of course we have a national Social Security program, instituted in the 1930s, to which all working Americans contribute, but it serves as only a minimal pension system that most workers must supplement in order to avoid being poor when they retire. Most public-sector workers receive some form of employer-provided health insurance, although like many private-sector workers, they are increasingly forced to pay an ever larger portion of the monthly insurance premium and are otherwise made to absorb the increased costs of health care (it should be noted that the public sector comprises only about 16 percent of the labor force in the United States, and the percentage is dropping). Moreover, the declines in health and pension provisions have hit lower-waged workers especially hard.[33] If benefits continue to shrink, it can be anticipated that life expectancy in the United States, which is already shorter than in every major nation in Western Europe, will also decline further.[34]

Meanwhile, the United States is the only rich democracy (out of twenty OECD countries) where workers actually work *more*, on average, over the course of a year, than they worked twenty years ago.[35] So while workers in the rest of the industrialized world have seen their annual hours of work *reduced* by an average of 215 hours during the past two decades, Americans are working 32 hours *more* now than they did then.[36] An important reason for the difference has to do with the fact that the average annual vacation for a worker in the United States (where employers are not legally mandated to provide their employees with any vacation time, paid or unpaid) is only *sixteen days*, a figure that is less than the statutory minimum vacation in every European country, and a full half of the amount of legally mandated vacation time in France, Finland, Austria, Denmark, Spain, and Sweden.[37] Moreover, American workers are not only permitted less daily rest or break time at work than European workers are, but with the exception of certain categories of workers (airline pilots, truck drivers, and so on) American workers actually have no statutory right to rest time or to bathroom breaks whatsoever, and managements generally have the right to require mandatory overtime of workers, without any fixed legal cap on the maximum number of hours.[38] There is neither a sickness leave policy, paid or unpaid, nor a paid maternity leave policy. However, for the minority of Americans working in firms with fifty or more employees, there are thirteen weeks of *unpaid* maternity leave.[39]

Of course, even though there are so few social benefits mandated by the state, individual employers do provide a range of benefits in the United States. The crucial difference between the United States and Europe, however, is that whether American workers receive social benefits is a function of either the state of the labor market or the state of their collective power. In other words, one chief determinant of whether an employer offers specific benefits has to do with the relative tightness of the labor market at any given time or place, or in any given occupation (with regard to the ability to attract and retain employees with needed skills). The other is the organizational power of workers in relation to employers. The reason, therefore, why so many of the indicators with regard to the social conditions of labor are so negative is that in the United States one problem serves as a virtual precondition for all the others: the system of labor relations overwhelmingly favors employers.

UNIONS AND THE PRIVATE SYSTEM OF SOCIAL PROVISION IN AMERICAN SOCIETY

For the tens of millions of workers in the United States who lack professional or managerial status, a union membership card is the principal passport to social citizenship. Whereas in Europe a more or less full complement of social benefits is granted on the basis of citizenship status, in the United States most social benefits are granted largely on the basis of union membership status.[40] Thus, through much of the postwar period American workers in the heavily unionized core sectors of the industrial economy were able to maintain a menu of social benefits that were comparable with (though never fully equal to) those granted to most Europeans as a right of citizenship. In Europe, in other words, there is a *public* system of social provision, created through legislation and financed by all employers and taxpayers, while in the United States there is a *private* system of social provision, which is limited principally to those who work in unionized companies. This private system of social welfare covers a diminishing proportion of workers because union density has dropped so precipitously in the United States (it is currently under 14 percent). However, the problem is not simply the low percentage of workers who are union members in the United States, but that it is almost as difficult to attain union membership status in the United States as it is to attain citizenship status in much of Europe, and once union status is attained it must be constantly defended against aggressive employer opposition.

When plants close down and jobs are lost in Europe, it is a situation that often triggers early and direct state intervention, so that workers and their families tend to be compensated and supported by a variety of social programs. There is little for American workers when their companies close and they lose their jobs.[41] Usually there is no mandated severance pay package or financial compensation from the state or the company for the community (apart from "unemployment insurance" to individual workers, which is normally thirteen weeks of cash payments). Furthermore, the requirement for advanced notice to workers that their workplace will close has only been in place since 1998. Prior to that, it was not uncommon that workers were informed on a Friday afternoon not to bother to report for work on Monday, since the plant would no longer be in operation. Even today, when workers are laid off or dismissed they are often simply handed their "pink slip" with no notice whatsoever, a cold-heartedness whose function is to enable the company to avoid spontaneous acts of sabotage or other expressions of unpleasantness.

It is to this situation that Alan Greenspan (the powerful chairman of the Federal Reserve Board) refers when he celebrates the low cost of dismissing workers and the ease by which it is accomplished in the United States, relative to Europe, where labor market "rigidities" supposedly result in smaller returns on investments in information technologies.[42] This is the standard

"European malaise" argument, often mentioned in the U.S. press, a socioeconomic malady that is somehow thought to be caused by shorter workweeks, universal health care, paid maternity leave, a livable minimum wage, and other basic social benefits. Although demonstrably incorrect in an objective sense (referred to by one skeptic as "a fairy tale as widely believed by our journalists as it is beloved by the businessmen who sign their checks"), the cry of "Eurosclerosis" is nevertheless a thoroughly understandable position for Wall Street to invoke as a means of quieting any noise for improved social benefits *at home*.[43]

Indeed, when we consider the situation of Americans "at home" in a literal sense, we confront such conditions as a lack of paid maternity leave, a child care system that is unsystematic and frequently unaffordable, a powerful stigma placed on the poor who seek state assistance and a growing pressure to privatize virtually all public activities, including the public retirement system. It is clear that the United States is on course, "full steam ahead," toward the creation of a system of "cradle to grave" neoliberalism whose highest moral teaching amounts to little more than an exhortation to the young to either "sink or swim."

For example, in contrast to the substantial investment in early childhood care made by European states to support the entry of women into the workforce, child care in the United States has remained an overwhelmingly private, rather than a public responsibility and, except for the provision of certain subsidies and social programs for the very poorest families, has been developed according to basic market principles. What this has produced for many American workers and their families is a serious cluster of social problems manifested most commonly in the twin crises of "latch-key kids" (the difficult situation whereby millions of children return home from school every day to an empty house, without adult supervision) and of the steep costs of child care, which the U.S. Census Bureau has ranked as the third largest household expense for families with young children, just after food and housing.[44] It is not entirely uncommon for a working-class parent, who may be earning $2,500 per month or less, to be forced to quit his or her job in the summer months when the school year has ended, simply because full-time child care for two children can easily cost one-half of a monthly paycheck.[45]

Overall, and in contrast to European models of universal social provision, American social welfare is deliberately stigmatizing. It is limited to the very poorest sectors of the population, benefits are provided only for a limited duration ("two years and out"), and it offers relatively little to help people to acquire the kinds of resources (job training, education, social networks, and reliable, affordable child care) that would make it possible to establish themselves in the more stable regions of the labor market. In short, it tends toward a punitive rather than an ameliorative system, functioning primarily as a disincentive against exit from the low-wage end of the labor market.[46] An important element that allows such conditions to be sustained is a curiously persistent system of beliefs in which one's social position is almost universally attributed to one's luck or one's individual character (of which one's individual work ethic is central). Thus the difficult social conditions that one might experience are widely viewed as the product of a "bad attitude," rather than recognizing the conditions themselves as a social product. The result is a situation in which, at least conceivably, one could be *less well off* (both materially and in psychic terms) while *employed* at a minimum-wage job in the United States than if one were *unemployed* in most

European countries. Both would represent almost equal deprivation on a material level. However, the unemployed European would likely be able to enjoy a greater sense of social well-being, with guaranteed health insurance, subsidized transportation and housing, and widely available public cultural institutions and activities, while feeling somewhat less socially stigmatized than if one were among the "working poor" in the United States.[47]

With regard to social provision, then, the contrasts between much of Europe and the United States are quite significant. In the United States social benefits primarily depend on either the state of the labor market or on the relative collective power of workers within a particular region or industry at a particular historical moment, while in Europe social benefits tend to be statutory and universal. Benefits can be more easily taken back in the United States than they can in a situation where they are firmly institutionalized and are enjoyed across an entire population. That is, as labor markets loosen in the United States, companies can afford to allow their benefit packages to shrink, and when employers feel emboldened (by loosened labor markets, by favorable shifts in the legal or political environment, or by their own organizational capacities) benefits that had been contractually granted to workers in a previous period of collective bargaining can be taken back in a subsequent one. This is never simple or easy, but in recent decades it has become absolutely routine.

Another important difference between the United States and Europe is that in the United States there is a highly decentralized system of collective bargaining and labor relations in which union representatives and employers negotiate at many thousands of unionized workplaces across the country, producing thousands of separate labor contracts that generally only apply and are only enforceable within each of the specific workplaces or firms alone. Trade union membership is a status that is attained (and maintained) workplace by workplace and firm by firm, through a process of quasi self-organization in which groups of workers, aided by representatives of one of sixty-five autonomous national union organizations (with loose jurisdiction over specific industries and occupations) mobilize an electoral campaign with the goal of convincing a majority of their coworkers to vote for union membership, on a collective basis, usually through a government-supervised "union-representation election." If successful, a local branch of the national union organization will be chartered as the officially sanctioned bargaining agent for the workers in that establishment.

Generally, individual unions negotiate with individual firms, maintaining a substantial degree of autonomy, both organizationally and politically. One implication of this is that while contract settlements may be able to be tailored to a particular situation facing specific workers and firms, there are no formal coordinating mechanisms. Pay differences between similar kinds of workers doing the same job tend to be high, and in general the distribution of wages for workers of the same age, education, gender, and occupation is much wider in the United States than in countries where wage bargaining is centrally coordinated.[48] In many European countries, by contrast, the results of collective bargaining are routinely extended throughout the industry, often by labor ministers, regardless of the number of union members, thus broadening and deepening the institutional presence of trade unions in the society.

For this reason union density figures can have different implications in different countries. Union density is relatively low in both France and the United States, for example, but in France, the social benefits won by French workers in heavily unionized industries radiate outward to the benefit of the workforce as a whole. Social benefits in the United States, by contrast, do not radiate far at all and must constantly be negotiated, renewed, and defended. Consequently, it is essential that U.S. unions keep organizing, not only to extend trade union rights but also to maintain them in the face of antiunion practices by employers. The broad menu of social benefits available to all citizens in European countries is only available to union members in the United States, and only when they have been wrested from the employer.

Although these differences might seem insignificant, what appear to be minor organizational differences actually represent fundamentally different concepts underlying trade unionism in the United States and Europe. In the United States unions have tended to be institutions representing their members, while in Europe they have tended to be institutions "representing the working class in society as a whole."[49] By agreeing to the principle that the union's purview is limited to the interests of the members within the firm, rather than the working class in the society, American unions have largely undercut any moral legitimacy they might have had in relation to a more generalized social solidarity. In other words, early in historical terms, but not without recurring political struggle over it, unions in the United States have largely relinquished the call to act on behalf of a "working class," accepting instead a much more limited role of voicing the interests of their particular members.

Certain limitations inhere in the process of union formation, which is based on an electoral model unknown in Europe.

Typically, for a union to be recognized the majority of workers within an enterprise must vote to form a local branch of a national union in an election supervised by the National Labor Relations Board (NLRB). However, the electoral model is less a natural outgrowth of democracy or of an American cultural predisposition toward individualism than it is a model imposed in the postwar period to displace worker militancy away from the workplace, the site of the very indignities that tend to lead workers to struggle for unionization in the first place.[50] Conflict is systematically channeled so that what may have begun as a spark of collective action for workers on the shop floor is quickly extinguished by the soporific of bureaucratic procedure and legal interpretation. In certain respects, industrial bureaucracy may therefore be considered "class warfare by other means."

Although workers have a legal right to organize a union, employers, particularly in the private sector, frequently contest unionization through aggressive antiunion campaigns that normally include the use of disinformation (in leaflets and in workplace "captive audience" meetings prior to the union election), through intimidation (threats to close the workplace, dismissal of union activists), and through endless legal maneuverings to delay resolution of the process (in order to demoralize union supporters and to replace them through attrition).[51] Even seemingly established unions can suddenly be subjected to ferocious and systematically developed campaigns of destabilization ("union busting") aimed at destroying unionism in the workplace and across entire industries. In comparative terms, unionization in the United States is a decentralized process, but one that is also intensely and openly in conflict. In recent decades the balance of power has shifted steadily and unambiguously toward employers to a degree that has put into question the very future of an institutionalized system of collective bargaining.

THE AMERICAN WORKER "DISAPPEARED"

Part of what makes it difficult to write about labor and the labor movement in the United States is that one is writing about something that inhabits only a microscopic place in the social imagination. It is probably no exaggeration to say that most Americans are about as unmindful of how labor "works" in the United States, as a system, as a process, and as a social grouping, as most non-Americans are. In important ways this can be taken as a measure of the success of the neoliberal social project, which ultimately depends on the virtual disappearance of the Worker, *at a symbolic level*, along with the simultaneous symbolic elevation of the Consumer, who has emerged to become the supreme subject and object of economic practice. That is, the Worker (a social actor whose interests were once identifiable and recognizable in a range of institutional forms) has gradually "disappeared" from the social imagination and has been replaced by the increasingly discernible figure of the Consumer (in whose name a host of traditional economic regulations have been methodically overturned).[52]

This shift has been expressed, on the one side, by a steady *inflation* of the social rights granted to the Consumer (for example, the "freedom" to choose, to obtain credit, to shop at all hours on any and every day, to have virtually anything delivered directly to one's door, with little waiting, and to generally be granted what appears to non-Americans as an absurd and unnecessary degree of "convenience" with respect to all phases of retail trade). On the other side, this has taken place at the expense of the systematic *dissolution* of the rights of the Worker (for example, the spread of contingency, wage decline, overwork, forced overtime, job surveillance, few mandated social benefits, erosion of the right to strike, sanctioned antiunionism, and so on).[53] It is not just a matter of these spheres standing in inverse proportion to one another, but that they are reciprocally generating conditions: on the other side of the smiling face of endless consumer "convenience" is the stern regime of coerced labor "flexibility."

American-based global retail giants like Toys 'R' Us, McDonald's, and Wal-Mart are essentially no more than high-volume, low-cost "selling factories" that are primarily fueled by a steady supply of inexpensive goods produced by cheap, international labor in the *manufacturing* phase, and then sold by contingent, low-wage, and nonunionized domestic workers in the hyperrationalized *retail* selling phase of the process. For example, with annual sales that top those of both General Motors and Exxon-Mobil, Wal-Mart has become a $220 billion-a-year empire and the number one retailer in the entire world.[54] It is so large that its effect has been not only to serve as a model for emulation by other retail corporations but also to serve as the primary force driving down labor costs through its direct coercive impact on the sixty-five *thousand* (65,000) companies that supply it with consumer goods.[55] That is, by demanding that its suppliers meet specified low costs, Wal-Mart exerts powerful downward pressure on wages and benefits across entire industries and regions. The four major pillars of Wal-Mart's success have been identified as its successful application of advanced technologies, its logistical flexibility, its reliance on imported goods, and its employment of nonunion labor; however, the conditions for the first three are essentially only made possible by the fourth, which creates the ability to manipulate a wholly unorganized labor force.

In response, one expects to hear the familiar refrain that "workers are consumers too" and that American workers therefore benefit from the mass-market consumer culture that Wal-Mart represents. Although workers certainly are able to purchase goods cheaply, instead of receiving higher wages that would allow them to pay a reasonable price for manufactured goods and services, Americans workers are expected to constantly scramble to seek ever cheaper goods (made by ever cheaper labor) in order to "compensate" for a quarter-century of wage stagnation, thus forcing them to act *as consumers* directly against their own group interests *as workers*. Yes, in the United States workers are indeed consumers too, so much so in fact that one could fairly say that the pressures on Americans to consume are almost as fierce as the pressures they face at work! In the United States the credit card industry sends out an incredible 2.5 *billion* solicitations annually, which compete for space in American mailboxes that are daily inundated with all manner of advertising brochures, promotional materials, and catalogues that sell an unimaginable variety of goods and services.[56] And the Internet, promoted as an "information highway," is actually evolving into a gigantic electronic billboard whose potential promotional capabilities will likely and very soon overwhelm the already thoroughly commercialized media domains of television and radio in the United States.

Meanwhile, within the realm of public discourse, economic policy has been largely stripped of any possible social entanglements, so that such questions as taxation, regulation, and deregulation tend to be debated and discussed as either technical matters or in terms of their effects on corporate profitability and behavior, with little attention to their broader social effects. In the mass media the economic health of the society is largely reduced to televised news reports on the ups and downs of the "Dow Jones industrial average" and the "NASDAQ Index" of stocks, an ubiquitous scorekeeping ritual that all Americans are obliged to follow despite the fact that 80 percent of American households have no direct stock holdings.[57]

In other words it represents a gauge that amounts to a distorted economic cardiogram because it misses what ought to serve as key vital signs of socioeconomic well-being, such as comparative living and working standards, real poverty levels, the ability of workers to organize (as well as any sense of all that is missed when one is forced to rely on official economic categories). Ironically, the wide transmission of stock market results tends to display, albeit implicitly and unintentionally, the class interests and struggles that are at play but that are normally unmentionable in American public discourse. One immediately thinks of the obvious conflicts of class interest that are revealed when the stock market goes up in response to a rising unemployment rate, and then sags as labor markets tighten and wages go up. Even while sometimes noting the irony, media commentators never pursue the implications that flow from the fact that interest rate adjustments (made by the Federal Reserve Bank to dampen the "threat of inflation") are often prompted by nothing more sinister than economic indicators that are judged to be *too favorable* to workers! As the established transmitter of all forms of "conventional wisdom" the mass media automatically advances the class-bound perspective that it is the risk of inflation and not unemployment that poses the greatest of economic dangers, a warning that is usually raised as a threat to consumers rather than to investors seeking to keep loan rates and labor costs as cheap as possible.

A crucial reason why employers have been able to so dominate the means of symbolic representation has largely to do with a labor movement that has not only failed to offer an oppositional voice within American society, in an ideological sense, but for most of the past half-century has been unwilling to represent itself as a labor *movement* at all. The formation of any group or movement is never a simple or even process of social representation, but is always uneven, is never fully formed, is in flux, in contention, and is also always partly allegorical.[58] Where social groups contend for power and influence in a hostile social universe (like unions in American society) they must constantly "demonstrate" their efficacy and potential, not only to those outside of the group or movement, but to the members of the group itself, whose cohesiveness and solidarity, whose very "groupness" must be constantly reinforced. "Demonstrations" therefore are just that, representational formations that demonstrate to participants and potential participants, friend and foe alike, not what a group "is" at any given time, but what it is potentially, with respect to mobilization, to commitment, to social disruption. In this sense a labor movement is known both by its forms of collective action and its organizational forms, as well as by the limits (both mental and institutional) that it imposes and that are imposed on action and organization.

In the postwar period the dominant representation of American labor has been that of a relentlessly pragmatic business unionism that has actively discouraged any expression of solidarity that might be construed as a threat to the existing order—that is, until very recently. In 1995, the American Federation of Labor—

Congress of Industrial Organizations (AFL-CIO), the federation that comprises nearly all the trade unions in the United States, held the first contested election for president since its formation more than a century ago. The election overturned a conservative, business-oriented union leadership that had proven itself utterly incapable of responding to more than two decades of a sustained antiunion assault by the corporations.

A triumvirate of militants who called themselves the "New Voice" replaced the old leadership. They won by promising to streamline the bureaucratic structure of the federation, to give labor a more visible and militant profile in the society, and to increase substantially the amount of energy and resources directed toward organizing new union members. Most significantly, they committed the American labor movement to the fight for social justice. Although the decentralized nature of American unionism necessarily limits the impact of a leadership change at the top of the AFL-CIO, it nevertheless represents a significant historical event. In part, the victory of the New Voice leadership means that for the first time those who are officially authorized to speak in the name of American labor are predisposed to do so in a way that is openly critical of the American style of neoliberal capitalism.

The position of dominance in the world attained by American-based corporations has largely been achieved because they have been able to operate from such a remarkably favorable position at home. With an acquiescent labor movement that has openly supported or mounted only insignificant opposition to policies of "military Keynsianism," to industrial deregulation, to the privatization of public services, and to a worldview in which the market represents the supreme arbiter of all human affairs, American corporations have grown accustomed to maneuvering in a domain with few significant constraints. "Freedom" is trumpeted so loudly and pressed so determinedly on the rest of the world because it promises the same reassuringly familiar conditions that have existed for business in the United States.

In the neoliberal utopia that corporations seek to create, there is no place for trade unions, making the future survival of a labor movement in the United States a very real and serious question. The reciprocally determining relationship that binds American capital and American labor, however, has meant that the same attempt to destroy the latter has spawned an extraordinary frontal challenge to the former, opening a world of new social possibilities. There is an enormous amount at stake, therefore, with regard to the future of the U.S. labor movement, not only for American society but for much of the rest of the world.

CHAPTER TWO

An Exceptionally Hostile Terrain

Pundits and scholars frequently talk and write about the American labor movement as if it has always been "exceptional" or different from the mass-based, radical labor movements of other advanced democratic countries in Western Europe. However, throughout much of the nineteenth century, observers would have noticed little that was unusual about American labor, at least in relation to France and England, two countries that were then at roughly comparable levels of capitalist development. The American labor movement was composed of skilled craft workers, whose political language and practices resembled those of their French and British counterparts.[1] This began to change only in the last quarter of the nineteenth century when, surprisingly, a broader, more radical labor movement began to take hold first in the United States. Indeed, in the mid-1880s commentators were characterizing the American working class as more advanced in terms of organization, militancy, and group consciousness. This state of affairs was not to last; by the time Werner

Sombart visited the United States at the turn of the twentieth century and penned his famous essay, *Why Is There No Socialism in the United States*, the American labor movement had become distinctive—not for being uniquely strong and class conscious— but instead for being weaker and more politically conservative than labor movements in Western Europe.[2] During the course of the next several decades, this distinctive narrowness would grow even more pronounced. Only in the late 1930s did American workers finally succeed in building strong, enduring unions that were a genuine economic and political force in the society. Yet the development of this relatively strong union movement never escaped the imprint of the forces that shaped its formative years and that continue to mold it today.

Those who portray the American labor movement as having *always* been weak and conservative frequently argue that the explanation for this lies in a failure of American working-class solidarity and combativeness (variously ascribed to affluence, or upward social mobility, or the existence of a vast territorial frontier, or early universal male suffrage, the two-party monopoly over political power, or the democratic tenor of everyday life).[3] Such a portrayal, however, is ahistorical and ignores those moments when American labor was decidedly unexceptional. It also mistakenly sees the properties of a social group as a simple product of the group itself, as if untouched by the social relationships in which the group is embedded. In particular, it takes no account of the mutually constituting relations between labor and capital and how these develop over time, including the ways in which state policies and political opportunities shape this relationship. Yet, in the United States, it has been American *employers*, especially, who have had the "exceptional" power to be able to create an exceedingly hostile terrain for labor, aided frequently by a state that openly intervened on their side rather than on the side of workers.

Like a fossil embedded in amber, the skeletal outlines of America's true labor exceptionalism can now be seen as having been deeply inscribed in the primal struggles of one late-nineteenth-century organization, the "Knights of Labor." First organized as a secret society by clothing workers in Philadelphia in 1869, "the Noble and Holy Order of the Knights of Labor" was a remarkably egalitarian organization that sought to organize all workers in America's heterogeneous labor force, regardless of skill level, nationality, race, or gender. The organization experienced a period of explosive growth in the early 1880s, largely fueled by a series of highly publicized strikes against the financier Jay Gould, a reviled national figure who symbolized and personified the evils of concentrated corporate power. By 1886, a year of considerable labor upheaval in the United States, the Knights had formed local assemblies in every state, had organized more than 700,000 members (close to 10 percent of the industrial labor force), and had begun to put forward its own members as candidates for local political office in dozens of communities across the country. Such dramatic growth, however, was followed by an equally spectacular decline; for within five years the Knights of Labor had collapsed as a viable national organization, effectively crippling working-class political mobilization in the United States for several generations.

As historically important as the Knights were as an organizational expression of indigenous social unionism, their real sociological significance has resided more in the cause of their death than in the way they lived. As Voss has systematically demonstrated elsewhere, the primary reason for the downfall of the Knights of Labor was a paradoxical result of their rapid growth and early success, which resulted in the mobilization of powerful *employers'* organizations.[4] Employers had at their disposal all of the benefits of rapid economic expansion and concentration to assist them in mobilizing against the Knights.[5] Even more importantly, in the United States of the 1880s, employers were given comparatively free reign. Unlike in England and France where the state intervened directly or behind the scenes to demand employer concessions, in the United States the government did nothing to constrain employers' actions.[6] By ignoring or minimizing both the truly "exceptional" power of American *employers*, as well as the mutually constituting *relations* between labor and capital (including a deregulated state operating on behalf of the latter) generations of analysts have tended to misconstrue the logic of American unionism as well as the real social character of American exceptionalism.

The downfall of the Knights played a crucial role in fixing the trajectory of twentieth-century trade unionism in the United States. Their defeat underscored the exceptional social power of employers and served to solidify the position of a much more conservative "business unionism" as a rival to the Knights' egalitarian social unionism. In other words, the defeat of the Knights served as a lesson that was hammered home by those who supported the moderate, pragmatic unionism of Samuel Gompers, president of the American Federation of Labor (AFL). Broad-based organizations and political radicalism were painted as dangerous and as sure paths to repression and defeat, while conservative nonradical politics were advocated as the best road to survival. The result was that the AFL's version of unionism—narrow, craft-based, and sectional—became firmly institutionalized, making it that much more difficult for successive generations to imagine or to accomplish a broader industrial and general unionism that might venture to represent a wider social constituency.

The simple lesson imprinted in the years following the Knights' defeat was unmistakable: broad-based organizing and radical politics would be soundly repressed. Consider events like the Pullman railroad strike of 1894, a widely known industrial action that was called by the socially inclusive American Railway Union and led by the renowned socialist Eugene V. Debs. After shutting down most of the nation's rail traffic when workers honored a boycott of cars made by the Pullman company, the union was utterly destroyed by a powerful employers' association that was successful in persuading state and federal troops to violently repress the strike. The troops killed 13 workers and arrested 705, including all the union leaders. Indeed, the use of state and federal troops to break strikes increased dramatically in this period: official records report that between 1886 and 1895, state militias were called out at least 118 times to put down labor unrest, often to protect strikebreakers.[7] Events like the Pullman strike reinforced the suspicions of noncraft and radical organizations within the AFL. Some leaders of the AFL referred to the American Railway Union as "the second edition of the Knights of Labor" and used its failed strike as a further lesson that sectional unionism and pragmatic politics were the only way for unions to survive in the hostile, antilabor terrain of the United States.

High walls were thus built around American trade unionism at the precise moment when the changing social composition of the American working class required a much broader organizational and ideological vehicle. By 1895 the pace of immigration accelerated dramatically; during the first decade of the new century proportionately more immigrants arrived than in any other decade in American history. With employers increasingly organizing work within the factories on the basis of ethnicity and language, their mostly southern and eastern European workforce was subdivided and segregated into various distinct occupational compartments.[8] Furthermore, ethnic segmentation went hand in hand with both a widening wage differential for skilled and unskilled work and a working class that was increasingly segregated in spatial terms, as the development of urban transport networks began to create "streetcar" suburbs for the more skilled segments of the working class (both native-born and older immigrant groups) while leaving the poorer unskilled workers and their families in ethnically homogeneous urban ghettos.[9]

Had the Knights survived, it is certainly arguable that the United States would have had a very different and much less exceptional century of labor history, a situation that might have had enormous national and international implications. At the very least, a working-class social unionism that was more deeply entrenched would have moderated the processes of ethnic fragmentation, favoring more inclusive classwide institutions that could have competed with exclusionary ethnic associations in the assimilation process of new immigrants.[10] As it was, the conservative craft-unionism of the AFL allowed for an intensified ethnic segmentation, by default, and also served as an institutional outpost of racist and nativist sentiment within the labor movement itself.[11]

The "pure and simple trade unionism" of the AFL became the overwhelmingly dominant institutional force in the labor movement throughout the first three decades of the twentieth century.

This brand of unionism also produced significant symbolic opposition to itself in movements like the Industrial Workers of the World (the "Wobblies," the IWW). Active from 1905 to its violent demise in 1917, the IWW was, as Paul Buhle has remarked in his study of business unionism, "everything that the AFL refused to be and did not wish to be."[12] The AFL proudly represented itself as the organizational expression of a select "labor aristocracy," while practicing a business-oriented pragmatism in its dealings with employers. In sharp contrast, the IWW practiced a revolutionary syndicalism that eschewed institutionalized "labor relations" entirely. Celebrating their marginal status in their theme song, "Hallelujah, I'm a Bum!" the Wobblies rode the rails from conflict to conflict, organizing the most marginal segments of the labor force (immigrants, the unskilled, migratory laborers), while readily "filling the jails" in struggles to assert their right to free speech. The Wobblies had no system for collecting membership dues, maintained no strike fund, rotated their officials to prevent the formation of organizational hierarchies (under the slogan, "We are all leaders"), and refused to sign labor agreements, the very basis of a collective bargaining system.[13] In other words, in refusing to act like a "responsible" trade union, or for that matter like an organization at all, the Wobblies can be seen as having been a relational product of its opposite, the relentlessly pragmatic business unionism of the AFL.

Like the Knights of Labor before them, the Wobblies' brief institutional existence served to demonstrate the extremely short life expectancy of radical unionism in the United States prior to the 1930s. In the aftermath of World War I, with a militant strike wave of four million workers beginning to wane, employer associations led by the National Association of Manufacturers and the U.S. Chamber of Commerce, and aided by the Justice Department of the U.S. government, the quasi-fascist American Legion, and even the AFL itself, mounted a ferocious campaign to break IWW strikes, to harass and deport its leadership and its immigrant followers, and to refine the process of the "red scare" campaign into a formidable ideological (and practical) armament in the defense of the social order.[14] Although the mythic status of the Wobblies would survive in the imagination of unionists and radicals for a long time, the kind of social unionism that they represented was swept from the stage in a dark night of political reaction and economic depression that enveloped the United States for almost two decades.

From out of this darkness would emerge in the 1930s the Congress of Industrial Organizations (CIO), a powerful movement of industrial unionism that remade the American labor movement. Three engines propelled the emergent CIO forward. The *first* was the Great Depression, which, while it wreaked massive social and economic havoc, also served to scrape away the legitimacy of American business. In the context of the Depression, the "Captains of Industry" and their political minions suddenly seemed completely bereft of answers to a catastrophe that would leave millions of newly unemployed to face the specter of starvation in a society with no system of state social provision. With its symbolic luster removed, business was suddenly incapable of offering a credible defense of the country's unbridled market economy, and it stood nakedly vulnerable to most forms of Marxist and social democratic criticism. The *second* principle factor that drove the rise of the CIO was a shift in the political field. In 1932 in the depths of the Great Depression, Franklin Roosevelt was elected president with substantial support from workers fed up with the government's inability to remedy massive unemployment and misery. Roosevelt soon cobbled together a plan for economic recovery that gave something to business, the allowance of legalized cartels to fight cutthroat competition, heretofore illegal in the United States, as well as something to labor, a requirement that employers had to acknowledge their workers' right to organize and to bargain collectively (detailed in Section 7a of the National Recovery Act). Although only a vague statement of policy that included no effective enforcement mechanism, the requirement had enormous psychological and political impact because it signaled that businessmen could no longer count on government backing to fight unionization. Workers began to feel a little less fearful of collective action, which was bolstered when the National Labor Relations Act (also known as the Wagner Act) was passed in 1935 and endorsed by the Supreme Court in 1937. This act strengthened workers' rights to form a union by setting up a government-monitored election system that at least in the early years favored CIO-style industrial unionism. The *third* force that propelled the CIO was a practical "culture of solidarity," nurtured by scores of communists, socialists, and Trotskyists hired by CIO leaders to organize the millions of relatively unskilled mass-production workers, regardless of race, gender, or citizenship status.

The CIO created permanent labor organizations throughout the mass-production industries of the United States, and it did so in a remarkably short period. Between 1933 and 1937, five million new members joined the union movement, and fully half of these were recruited in just a handful of months in 1937. Another four million were added to labor's ranks during the next decade, so that by the end of World War II, almost one-third of all workers were unionized, with a much higher proportion in the mass-production industries at the heart of the national economy.[15]

Perhaps more significant even than the numbers was the fact that the CIO changed the symbolic place of unions in the public imagination from organizations providing narrow protection for the market skills of privileged artisans, to a social movement embodying and pursuing social justice.[16] This was not, it must be added, a matter of the successful dissemination of the "party line" by leftist organizers, but rather was chiefly a product of tactics that built on and bolstered social solidarity.[17] General strikes that enveloped San Francisco, Minneapolis, and Toledo in 1934 were punctuated by open and brutal class warfare, providing an unmistakably clear representation of the sort of "class analysis" that the radicals who led these uprisings had been attempting to convey in ideological terms. In 1936 and 1937, moreover, hundreds of thousands of workers throughout the industrial belt, from Akron, to Flint, to Chicago, to Philadelphia, to New York, as well as in many other cities, engaged in sympathy strikes and sit-down strikes (factory occupations) to "organize the unorganized!" as the slogan went, capturing the public imagination, while revealing precisely the ways in which employers were vulnerable to the tactical leverage of workers.[18] Thus, sit-down strikes demonstrated repeatedly their effectiveness in overcoming a half-century of employers' strikebreaking strategies. The integrated nature of production lines meant that a disciplined group of militants could close a plant and prevent strikebreakers from getting to the machines, a prospect further foreclosed by the mobilization of thousands of strike supporters to create mass picket lines around the plants, thus preventing or slowing any attempt to clear the workers out. Sit-down strikers enjoyed a clear tactical advantage, both because of their intimate knowledge of the plant interior and because management feared damage to the machinery in an assault on the strikers.[19]

However, this tactical advantage alone would not have been enough to overcome business opposition to workers' demands for greater democracy at work had it not been for the government's refusal to repress the dramatic sit-down strike against General Motors in 1937. Flint was a company town par excellence: four out of every five workers were employed by GM, and the mayor, police chief, three city commissioners, the head of the radio station, the editor of the newspaper, and school officials were all on the GM payroll. In the past, corporate dominance like this would have made it easy for a powerful company like GM to call on the local police and state militia to deliver the death blow to strike activity, especially a sit-down strike of questionable legality. However, in 1937, neither the governor of Michigan nor Franklin Roosevelt were willing to deploy the national guard or the army to remove the strikers. As a result, General Motors suddenly reversed long-standing policies and agreed to recognize the autoworkers' union. U.S. Steel and Chrysler, two other giant corporations at the center of the national economy, soon followed suit.[20]

In the wake of the GM settlement, nearly five million workers took part in some form of industrial action. Often these actions brought entire working-class communities into the heat of battle as women's auxiliaries and community groups mobilized in support of the strikers. The AFL response to the extraordinary militancy of industrial unionism was telling. Seeking to take advantage of the changed political environment, the AFL had initially sponsored the industrial union movement, but it soon withdrew support in the face of CIO militancy. In August 1936, the AFL executive council suspended several of the CIO unions that it had itself set into motion and later expelled them for being "communist dominated." For most of the next decade, it fought the CIO tooth and nail, both organizationally and politically. This despite the fact that by the end of 1937 the wave of militancy inspired by the emergence of industrial unionism had caused the membership of the fledgling CIO unions to jump fourfold and had also brought a million new members into the old AFL unions as well.[21]

The political character of the CIO can be seen to have been expressed as much in its forms of mobilization as in the ideological and political commitments of its leadership (although these were obviously related), for it was through sympathy strikes, sitdown strikes, and a series of regional general strikes it had mobilized that its differences from the AFL were most clearly demarcated. That is, in a struggle that prefigured its objective, the cultures of solidarity formed to accomplish very practical tasks and objectives represented, in practice, an unambiguous opposition to the existing order, thus creating the context for a symbolic struggle against capitalism. In a society in which the forces of anticapitalism have been prevented from sustaining any meaningful institutional existence, this must be recognized as having represented a significant political achievement.

In any event, at the height of its militancy in the decade of the 1930s, the CIO can be seen as having been a labor movement that was decidedly unexceptional. Moreover, it was the moment in the history of American social provision when the broad political coalition that delivered labor legislation also delivered national social legislation, the Social Security Act of 1935, which might very well have been the basis for a full-fledged system of public social insurance, along Western European lines.

TAMING INDUSTRIAL UNIONISM

The outline of the story of postwar American labor was scripted in and by the Second World War itself, because the wartime "national emergency" served as both context and fulcrum for a drive to dampen the militancy of American workers and the solidarism of industrial unionism. Successfully waging a world war on foreign soil required a massive expansion of domestic productive capacity and thus the mobilization of an enormous labor effort. The fervency of the patriotic call to national unity against the Axis threat provided powerful ideological support for a series of "temporary" institutional reforms that would later come to serve as the archetype for the postwar system of labor relations.

Government intervention in labor relations occurred on an unprecedented scale during the war, taking the form of a series of emergency measures that, retrospectively, can be seen to have prefigured (and shaped) important aspects of postwar American unionism. First, a significant process of co-optation occurred by which labor leaders were appointed to positions of authority, alongside business and military leaders, on a series of tripartite boards governing wartime labor relations. Not only were the labor leaders who served on the National Defense Mediation Board and the War Labor Board (many of whom had started as immigrants and rank-and-file shop workers) suddenly the recipients of significant personal social status and authority, but also their unions (both industrial and craft) were consecrated with an altogether new level of official, institutional legitimacy. At the same time, their actual say over the administration of war production was relatively limited, and although many hoped that the wartime measures might set the stage for national-level bargaining after the war, for the duration their role was primarily to lend legitimacy to councils that were designed to monitor and restrict any labor activities that might disrupt war production.[22]

The second crucial wartime "reform," therefore, was to end all strike activity for the duration of the war effort. Even before the War Labor Board had been established to facilitate disputes "by peaceful means" (which meant compulsory arbitration) the entire executive council of the AFL and the leaders of one hundred AFL unions had already voted for a no-strike policy. The CIO leadership followed by issuing no-strike pledges at each of its annual conventions, a position it defended by emphasizing the honor of contributing to the war against fascism in the face employer provocation, profiteering, and appeasement.[23] The no-strike pledge was defended, then, as an expression of the class struggle, rather than as an abandonment of it.

In return, the unions were granted a modicum of institutional security that allowed them to add some four million new members during the war, but this did little to alleviate problems for workers on the shop floor. Like most Americans, workers strongly supported the war effort. Had they been given the opportunity to endorse their leaders' no-strike pledge, they probably would have, but sharply deteriorating conditions in the workplace goaded them into engaging in an unprecedented number of "wildcat" strikes (unofficial, usually brief, spontaneous strikes mounted by workers to deal with shop-floor problems during the term of a union contract) during the war years, thus "setting a new pattern of industrial unrest" as two analysts noted at the time.[24] The gap between belief and action was less a contradiction than it might have seemed, especially from the vantage point of the shop floor where all sacrifice for "national unity" was expected from the workers, while company profits reached an all-time high, growing 250 percent above prewar levels, and while wages were frozen and most worker grievances were ignored or tied up in the bureaucratic machinery of the War Labor Board. By the end of the war, the frenzied "war for production" had produced more than *ten times* the number of Americans who were injured on the job compared to those who were injured fighting the war: production lines had been dangerously sped up and basic safety regulations routinely bypassed.[25]

Wartime industrial measures accomplished several crucial precedents that would come to shape the character of postwar unionism. First, a bureaucratic system of grievance resolution was imposed for settling industrial conflict, a new "industrial jurisprudence" that was closely bound within a framework of commitment to maintain production at all costs.[26] Secondly, the emergency industrial measures served to widen the social and experiential gulf between rank-and-file workers and a union leadership that had drawn closer to management, that seemed ready to embrace its newfound institutional legitimacy, and that had shown its willingness to exercise its authority over the union membership. Although not immediately obvious at the close of the war, the effects of these processes became evident soon enough.

With its potential European competitors decimated by the war and heavily in debt, and at the peak of its productive capacity, the United States seemed to emerge from WWII in an enviable position. The prewar prophecy of an "American Century" could no longer be dismissed as mere adolescent overconfidence; now the conditions for its realization appeared completely self-evident. But despite appearances, two very serious problems remained for American capitalism, summarized by the head of the General Electric Corporation, Charles E. Wilson, on his entry into the administration of President Truman as "Russia abroad, labor at home." The first was rooted in the considerable influence and respect enjoyed by the Soviet Union after the defeat of Hitler, especially in southern and eastern Europe, and the obvious long-term threat that this posed to an American capitalism anxious to dominate international markets. The second problem reflected a general breakdown of managerial control in American industry, a process that had been sparked by the militant formation of the CIO in the late 1930s, that had continued during the war in wildcat strikes that disrupted war production, and that was brought into sharp relief by a massive postwar strike wave that punctuated the new situation on the shop floor. For businessmen in the United States, this situation was uniquely intolerable: as comparative research makes clear, American managers are more fiercely committed to managerial prerogatives than are their European counterparts, who had learned to accept class politics and state involvement in the employment relationship in the nineteenth century.[27] As wartime controls were being lifted, it seemed to many American employers that the worker militancy that had confronted them prior to the war had only become more deep-rooted in the intervening years, and that they faced a serious and ongoing threat.[28]

In important respects, the cold-war fusillade of anticommunism provided a key to the solution of both problems. Although directed at various segments of the society, from military and government functionaries, to academics and artists, nowhere was the effect of "McCarthyism" more damaging in institutional terms than in the labor movement.[29] A special weapon fashioned for this assault was the Taft-Hartley Act, passed in 1947. Drafted by a team of corporate lawyers and shepherded through the legislative process by a compliant Congress, the act's goal was much broader than simply the elimination of communists from the labor movement: it was intended to repeal those provisions in the earlier National Labor Relations Act that had proven beneficial to the labor movement throughout the previous decade.

The Taft-Hartley Act had a remarkably broad scope and brought to a halt any hopes that labor might achieve either national-level bargaining or an expanded system of social provision. At its most basic level, Taft-Hartley weakened union security in three important ways. First, it made the union certification process much less flexible and responsive to labor than it had under the Wagner Act. To accomplish this, it eliminated many of the nonelection, informal methods the National Labor Relations Board had earlier used to determine whether a majority of workers favored union representation. It also granted employers new "free-speech" rights during the election period, providing an opportunity for employer resistance to unionization and a decertification procedure that has no parallel in Europe.[30] These changes in the recognition process had the effect of making the union presence in any firm more tenuous and contested than it had been, and it greatly enlarged the role of government functionaries, management advisors, lawyers, and legal hairsplitting in the process of union formation. All the effervescence of the collective dynamic, with its capacity to generate wonderment, creativity, and group solidarity among participants (and therefore the source of its strength), would now give way to regulation, individuation, and atomization that are the inevitable products of judicial proceedings, electoral procedures, and the systematic delegation of authority to those of higher rank. Additionally, Taft-Hartley encouraged workers to directly file individual grievances with management, largely circumventing their elected union representatives on the shop floor. Moreover, in order to limit further erosion of managerial control over the production process, foremen (who are supervisory employees on the shop floor) were prevented from joining or forming unions. (This provision prevents huge numbers of white-collar and service sector employees, including low-wage, fast-food "managers" and registered nurses with even minor supervisory duties, from unionizing.)

Second, it outlawed the "closed shop," which had the effect of loosening union influence and shifting control over labor markets to employers.[31] Third, it permitted individual states to pass laws further restricting union security within their borders, thus creating the legal basis for a union-free haven within the United States and allowing corporations to avoid or to flee the unionization of their enterprises. Since 1947, twenty states, mostly in the South and West, have passed these "right-to-work" laws that make unionism extremely difficult to maintain. The domestic equivalent of a "banana republic," the right-to-work states comprise a massive region of the country to which American corporations have long been able to move their operations in pursuit of an unregulated, unorganized, and, consequently, low-wage-paying business climate.[32]

As significant as these changes would be, perhaps the most far-reaching consequence of the Taft-Hartley Act was that it accomplished what amounted to the unilateral disarmament of labor.

The act so severely constrained the ability to mobilize strikes that such actions were drained of much of their potency as weapons of collective resistance. Sympathy strikes and secondary boycotts, two proven weapons of union solidarity that had been used to such powerful effect in the building of the CIO, were outlawed. The president of the United States was granted the power to intercede in strikes with the right to impose a mandatory eighty-day "cooling-off" period, thus formally enlisting the president in the strikebreaking process.[33] In addition, the law greatly strengthened the hand of employers during strikes by giving strikebreakers the right to vote in union-representation elections, while providing an extraordinary legal mechanism whereby strikebreakers who had replaced strikers in a workplace could actually petition for an election to "decertify" the existing union, one whose picket lines they had crossed! Further, by making available to employers the option of seeking legal injunction against mass picket lines, a judicial mechanism was provided to limit any effective resistance to strikebreakers in the first place!

Under the terms of the act, union leaders were to be held liable for not actively opposing wildcat strikes. Suddenly, union leaders would be fined and arrested for failing to act as disciplinarians of the membership, thus further institutionalizing the distance between the leadership and the rank and file.[34] The intent was to confer increased control on leaders who could be expected to be less militant than the unrestrained rank and file, while institutionally strengthening the more tepid forms of union practice.

Anticommunist provisions were also central to the law, representing an assault on the radicalism that had played such a significant role in the struggles that built the CIO and that continued to animate the internal life of the industrial unions.[35] Under the terms of Taft-Hartley, union officials at all levels were required to sign an anticommunist "loyalty oath." (Not so their employers!) This requirement effectively placed an entire generation of labor leaders on the defensive for their actions and associations over the course of the previous decade, the 1930s, while subjecting them to charges of perjury for those actions, words, or associations that could be construed as signifying communist affiliation.

Union leaders' initial response to the Taft-Hartley Act was to urge noncompliance. The great miners' leader John L. Lewis denounced it as "the first ugly, savage thrust of Fascism in America," and sporadic mass demonstrations were held to protest it. But although CIO leaders refused to sign the loyalty oaths when they were first enacted, they soon realized that failure to sign could result in the devastation of their unions. Refusal meant that any government protections with regard to union rights would be withdrawn, not only leaving unions completely vulnerable to corporate antiunion practices, but also barring any noncompliant union from appearing on a labor board election ballot, now the primary way of gaining union recognition.

Fratricidal warfare within the union movement proved to be an equally important factor limiting opposition to Taft-Hartley, as various ideological factions and blocks within unions found that they could rely on the anticommunist provisions of the law to purge radicals who posed a challenge within their own unions, while the communist-led unions were suddenly more vulnerable than ever to raids by rival unions seeking to expand their membership. In the context of the national hysteria of "McCarthyism," some individual CIO unions actually came to embrace the anticommunist provisions of the act in order to win members from the "red unions." Thus, within five years after the leadership of the communist-led United Electrical Workers (UE) had first refused to sign the loyalty oath, an anticommunist rival, the International Union of Electrical Workers (IUE) had been chartered and, along with scores of other unions, was busy dividing up the original jurisdiction of the UE.

Retrospectively, it is hard to imagine a more devastating judicial assault. The Taft-Hartley Act went a long way toward limiting the presence of unions in postwar American society (union membership never rose above the 35 percent of the labor force that was attained in 1955), thus cutting off the path taken by the German labor movement when it used its growing social power to create permanent structures of tripartite representation and, eventually, a generous system of public social provision. Taft-Hartley also de-fanged the strike, thus sharply delimiting the *kind* of unionism that could be practiced in the United States and effectively cutting off the path pursued by the postwar French labor movement, which relied on mass solidarity and militancy to build and protect a system of public social provision. In contrast to both the German and French unions, the U.S. labor movement was largely stripped of its ability to act like a social movement.

Throughout the war and the immediate postwar period, unions in the United States had pushed for legislation that would expand the system of social provision begun by the Social Security Act of 1935, as organized labor sponsored legislation in 1943 and 1945 that would have created national health insurance in the United States (such as the Wagner–Dingell–Murray bills). And labor strongly supported the Full Employment Bill of 1945, which would have established a right to employment for all

Americans. After losing those battles and failing to overturn Taft-Hartley, unions increasingly looked to collective bargaining to attempt to gain things like medical benefits, pensions, and employment security. The extent of labor's parochialism and depoliticization in the wake of Taft-Hartley was masked at first by talk on the part of some CIO leaders, like Walter Reuther, who sought to link collective bargaining over fringe benefits to a larger political strategy for gaining support for a generalized public system of social provision. He reasoned that if unions could push the cost of fringe benefits high enough, employers would eventually utilize their formidable social power to push for public social provision as a way of alleviating their financial burdens. However, pretty soon such rhetorical leftism was set aside in favor of a much more limited strategy of building a private system of social provision, incrementally, firm by firm.[36]

Thus Taft-Hartley served corporate interests well by accomplishing the near-total domestication of industrial unionism. However, this was also supported by certain forces within the trade union movement itself. In return for their complicity and their willingness to relinquish their most potent weapons, unions were granted a measure of stability and even modest growth in the postwar structure of American society.[37] A new "push-button unionism" characterized by an array of bureaucratic practices, from formal labor board elections, routinized grievance procedures, and automatic dues deductions, was enabled by Taft-Hartley, and it clearly appealed to those business unionists (particularly in the building-trades and other craft unions) who never had much stomach for the class struggle in any case, as well as to those leaders attracted to the high salaries, the generous "fringe" benefits, and the newly formed status of "labor statesman" that was attainable by the postwar labor leader. Within the context of sustained economic expansion and low unemployment, many union leaders were able to deliver steady wage increases to a growing membership in the decades following the war; in the face of this possibility few were inclined to continue bemoaning what Taft-Hartley had eliminated.

Meanwhile, American intellectuals in the postwar period tended to celebrate the tranquilized relationship between labor and capital, viewing it as an expression of a new "social contract," while largely ignoring the central role that Taft-Hartley had played in achieving it. By neglecting the coercive leverage of the law, practitioners of this overly optimistic sociology were able to declare a "new consensus" in a society in which class conflict had been overcome, an "end of ideology" had been achieved, and where the consumer had overtaken the producer as the supreme symbolic subject of "postindustrial" society. With the doctrine of "shared values" increasingly dominating the methods and models of American social science, the Taft-Hartley Act, although a clear expression of class conflict, was mistaken for an accord that signaled its transcendence.

Within the postwar intellectual universe, social facts and social fictions tended to circulate in a reciprocally confirming manner, so that a way of seeing society was created that conformed to that version of reality that was being imposed by society's most powerful interests. In an ideological and in a practical sense, the domestication of labor served as a basic precondition for both the expansion of the cold war and the explosion of American consumerism that accompanied it. Both built on a compliant labor movement that maintained the necessary industrial order (for the production of both weapons and durable consumer goods), while together they furnished a backdrop for the dogma of competitive individualism, providing a reasonably plausible facade of class-lessness on which it depended. After all, in the context of Mc-Carthyism the language of class struggle was literally "unspeakable" in the United States, and for most Americans who had endured nearly two decades of austerity, the postwar frenzy of mass consumption was experienced more as a demonstration of inclusion in the putative "American Dream" than as an expression of social differentiation. In the constructed imagination of postwar American capitalism, the "middle class" had emerged as the true "universal class," with the status of "middle-classness" made readily accessible through the acquisition of a menu of consumer goods (an automobile, a private house, and a full complement of household appliances).[38] While the language of consumer sovereignty was ascendant in the postwar period, poverty was largely absent from public discourse and consciousness, though the rate of poverty was considerable in postwar America.[39]

THE PRACTICES OF BUSINESS UNIONISM

In contrast to the AFL's traditional support for American imperial domination, for a brief instant the CIO seemed to provide a potential source of institutional opposition to U.S. imperial designs. But with passage of Taft-Hartley the hope of any genuine ideological independence soon faded, and in 1955, when the AF of L and CIO merged, both labor federations were in essential agreement about the role of the United States in the world. Throughout the postwar decades the AFL-CIO would not only provide ideological support to U.S. foreign policy (a stance virtually indistinguishable from support for U.S. corporate interests in the world) but also would itself become a key institutional operative in securing and maintaining U.S. dominance.

Through the "American Institute for Free Labor Development" (AIFLD), an organizational cover created to provide labor with working links to the CIA, the State Department, and relevant business interests, the American trade union movement became actively complicit in the suppression of militant or communist trade unionism everywhere, particularly in Latin America, where "counterinsurgency" characterized the relationship between the United States and an endless string of landowning oligarchs, *comprador* industrialists, and military chieftains, many created by the CIA. "Free labor" meant unions free of left-wing influence, and despite a smattering of protest from a handful of progressive unions in the United States (most notably in the latter stages of the Vietnam War and, later, in opposition to U.S. support for the barbarism committed in Central America in the 1980s), the AFL-CIO spent most of the period of the cold war as an enthusiastic cold warrior.

Struggles over the forms of collective action were an important arena of conflict between union leaders and rank-and-file militants. While union-sanctioned strikes continued, and even grew in number in the 1960s and 1970s, the effectiveness of strikes had been weakened by the provisions of Taft-Hartley and by reliance on a contract system of bargaining in which most union-management contracts forbid strikes "during the term of agreement." This eliminated the element of surprise, thus guaranteeing employers uninterrupted production during the contract period (often three or four years), while allowing them ample time to prepare for upcoming strikes. In contrast to the "official strike," which required sanction by the union leadership and which tended to emphasize wages and benefits, militants frequently mobilized wildcat strikes to resolve immediate problems faced by the rank and file on the shop floor (for example, production speedup, harassment by superiors, illegal firings, dangerous working conditions, and so on). Wildcat strikes are spontaneous actions, generated at the local level and outside the control of employers and union leaders. They create a difficult dilemma for the former, who wish to maintain uninterrupted production flows, and for the latter, who not only have a stake in the sanctity of the contract that they have negotiated and signed, but also are legally required to actively oppose them.

Such strikes occurred frequently in a range of industries, but particularly among coal miners, steelworkers, and autoworkers, in the decades following the war.[40] In important respects they can be seen to have represented a "practical critique" of the postwar "social contract," challenging both the bureaucratic system of labor relations and the business unionism that accompanied it. That is, wildcats acted as an alternative and more direct form of grievance resolution where the bureaucratic channels (which the union leadership was forced to defend) had become clogged or otherwise ineffective.[41] There were many examples, the most serious being the mining industry, where stalled grievance systems led to hundreds of wildcat strikes every year between 1950 and 1975. The most legendary case occurred at the General Motors plant in Lordstown, Ohio, in the early 1970s, where an accumulation of 20,000 grievances led to a sustained rank-and-file rebellion and embodiment of the expression "blue-collar blues," a term designating the high degree of industrial malaise that existed.

In a unionized workplace, a grievance is a formal complaint issued over a perceived violation of the union contract. Grievances are processed through a series of pyramidal steps, beginning with an informal exchange between the worker and supervisor on the shop floor and ascending from each "step" to a higher level of authority until the grievance is resolved. It is often a five-step process, and if there has been no resolution at step four, the grievance may conclude, often many years later and at a substantial monetary cost, with the appointment of a neutral arbitrator to settle it.

The sociological significance is that each step of the grievance procedure becomes more depersonalized than the previous one, and each removes the grievance further, in both spatial and temporal terms, from the context in which it was generated. It is a process that seeks, literally, to displace conflict, by channeling it away from those with an immediate and tangible stake in its resolution, to the desks of ever-higher grades of bureaucrats. But instead of such rule governance signifying the cessation of social conflict (as many social scientists had presumed) rank-and-file workers often experience the bureaucratic procedures as the "class struggle by other means," viewing the grievance system as a mechanism for delaying, postponing, or nullifying the resolution of problems on the shop floor, where management may simply find it more profitable to impede the settlement of a grievance than to resolve it promptly.

Their relatively spontaneous, democratic character makes wildcat strikes the direct inverse of bureaucratic grievance procedures, but they have also been capable of acquiring some degree of durability and organization. Groups of militants mobilized them to circumvent bureaucratic channels, while militant groupings were sometimes formed in their wake. Throughout the 1970s the leadership bodies of many of the largest trade unions were regularly challenged by dissident groups of steelworkers, miners, autoworkers (in particular, Black autoworkers), truck drivers, and postal workers, among others. Often formed at the local plant level, they sometimes developed a national presence representing a voice for militancy and democracy in unions that were corrupt and autocratic (the "Miners for Democracy" and the "Teamsters for a Democratic Union" have been well-known examples). Embodying many of the social-movement characteristics that had been discarded by the unions themselves, their willingness to give voice to radical sentiments were in sharp contrast to the unremitting probusiness rhetoric of the leadership. Such groups provoked sharp opposition, both from the existing union leadership deploying the resources of incumbency (for example, monopolizing the organs of internal communication, allocating resources to secure allegiance, and manipulating fears toward "outsiders," "reds," and so on), as well as from the corporations, for whom the dependability of a bureaucratized business unionism was much preferable to the militant unionism of rank-and-file dissidents.

Business unionism could be effective, however, especially during a period of economic expansion and according to the rather narrow framework that its leaders were willing to accept. By limiting itself to the wages and benefits of its members, and by committing itself to the general goals of American-style capitalism rather than to a radical agenda of social reform, at a national level the postwar labor movement provided corporations with a measure of domestic stability and predictability in a period of economic expansion. In return, unions were granted a degree of institutional security in high-growth sectors of the economy with an opportunity to negotiate steady wage and benefit gains for their members.

At the industry-level, stability could be achieved in one of two ways. In industries dominated by just a few large firms, like the automobile and steel industries, wage agreements were set by the practice of "pattern bargaining," in which wage settlements reached at one firm became the pattern for agreements throughout the industry, thus eliminating wages as a factor in competition. The same result was produced when unions served as work contractors supplying skilled labor to employers, as in the case of the building-trades unions that furnished skilled contract labor to firms in the construction industry. This process tended to maintain wage stability in the market over time, to the benefit of both union members and the many small construction contractors who relied on their skilled labor. It was the stability produced by such monopoly arrangements that served as the source of strength for what Daniel Bell considered a distinctly American "market unionism."[42]

As a result the American worker experienced a sustained period of economic progress. Thus average hourly earnings of manufacturing production workers rose by 81 percent between 1950 and 1965, the heart of the postwar economic boom (more importantly, the real, spendable weekly earnings of a production worker with a family of four rose 31 percent in the same period). Nonmonetary benefits (health benefits, pensions, vacation and sick days, and so on) rose from 17 percent of the value of compensation for a manual laborer in 1951 to more than 50 percent in some of the largest industrial firms by 1981.[43]

In the nation's basic manufacturing industries (auto, steel, electrical equipment, rubber, and so on), where rates of unionization approached 100 percent, unions were essentially able to negotiate for their members an American equivalent of the

European "social wage." Although limited in scope (to unionized workers in certain core industries) as well as in depth (they never attained the social reach of Scandinavian-style family- and child-support mechanisms), these contracts demonstrated the power of business unionism to deliver the goods under the right economic circumstances. At the same time, it was a system that amplified inequality, for workers outside the unionized core of the economy had only meager social provision and, typically, much lower wages. Relatively high levels of compensation were sustained for several decades for autoworkers, truck drivers, steelworkers, meatpackers, among others, through pattern bargaining. However, by the end of the 1960s this began to change, as European and Japanese manufacturers began to make headway into markets long dominated by American business, and companies came under increasing pressure to squeeze more out of their domestic operations. Pattern agreements were weakening and the "wage escalator" that was being ridden by unionized workers had stalled and was beginning its descent. For the family of an individual worker, the 1970s was a decade characterized by a steady erosion of purchasing power, as workers were forced to work more overtime hours and forced to increasingly rely on income from other family members, in addition to taking on increasingly high levels of installment debt in order to forestall the decline in living standards.[44]

SHREDDING THE POSTWAR
SOCIAL CONTRACT

It is hard to imagine more favorable circumstances for doing business than those that prevailed in the decades following the war. Supported by an expanding economy, a compliant labor movement had essentially ensured that there would be no serious domestic challenge to capitalist goals, thus allowing corporations the freedom to roam the world in search of profits (with the ready support of an immense military apparatus whose charge it was to make the world safe for capitalism!). Then later, as the economy contracted, instead of mobilizing significant opposition to the threats of layoffs and plant closings, a union leadership that had been well schooled in the language of the social contract could do little but accept, however grudgingly, the rationale advanced by employers and their agents, that concessions by labor were necessary to stem the tide of industrial decline.

A palpable unease had developed, it should be recalled, within the "higher circles" of American society in the 1970s. The myth of American military invincibility was cracking in Vietnam, the vulnerability of Western Capitalism was exposed by the oil crisis of 1973, and the nation's core political, judicial, and media institutions were deeply shaken by the Watergate crisis. Although these represented hard shocks to the "national consciousness," what was less dramatic, but equally unsettling was the successful incursion into American domestic markets (as well as international markets once dominated by American firms) of "foreign"-made goods, from automobiles, to electronic consumer products, to new technologies. Made visible by a shamelessly nationalistic mass media, the successes of "foreign" industrial competition raised serious doubts about the Fordist utopia of a perfect circle of production and consumption. Business leaders became determined to accomplish a shift in the balance of power. It would not be simple, as the magazine *Business Week* counseled in 1974: "It will be a hard pill for many Americans to swallow—the idea of doing with less so that big business can have more. . . . Nothing that this nation, or any other nation, has done in modern economic history compares in difficulty with the selling job that must now be done to make people accept the new reality."[45]

By the decade of the 1980s, the basic customs governing collective bargaining in the United States had undergone a remarkable transformation. Employers now eagerly approached the collective-bargaining process as a means of winning back from labor the security and the benefits that had been achieved by earlier generations of workers. Whether they could make a plausible case for "competitive pressure," companies of all description soon realized how easy it was to loot the store of contractual rights that unions had accumulated, simply by threatening to close the shop. In the process, workers' expectations were forced downward by the humiliating spectacle of once-solid union contracts being reopened and emptied in front of their eyes under the imminent threat of job loss.

In the recession of 1980–83, in industry after industry, employers took advantage of heightened unemployment levels to demand massive contract concessions. From the makers of agricultural implements, aluminum, automobiles, buildings, glass, newspapers, oil, processed meats, rubber, steel, to airlines, mine owners, supermarket chains, trucking companies, to local and regional governments and school districts, came demands for wage cuts, wage and pension freezes, reduction or elimination of automatic cost-of-living adjustments, and the establishment of permanently lower pay scales for newly hired workers.[46] This was a *scala mobile* in reverse, whereby most employers not only demanded wage concessions but also used the economic recession to raid established contract components like vacation time and paid holidays, while effectively eliminating thousands of jobs by changing long-standing work rules on staffing levels and job classifications. As the recession came to a close the traditional systems of pattern bargaining that had prevailed throughout the postwar decades, binding together the most highly unionized groups of workers within and across industries and sustaining reasonably high standards of living, were in complete disarray. With the breakdown in this system of industry-wide standards, employers were much freer to turn the screws, pitting workers in one company against those in another, one plant against another, one work group against another, one worker against another.

Like ostriches with their heads in the sand, most union leaders maintained the public position that the wave of concessions was an inevitable (and temporary) result of a normal downturn in the business cycle. Their commitment to the postwar system of labor relations simply would not permit them to admit or even to perceive that employers were tearing up the social contract and were actually engaged in a fight for the ultimate concession—the complete destruction of union representation.

Although it was already well underway, to the media and the public the employer offensive against the unions was signaled in 1981 by President Ronald Reagan's brazen assault on the air traffic controllers' union, the Professional Air Traffic Controllers Organization (PATCO). Within several months of assuming office, while trumpeting slogans of national renewal ("It's morning in America"; see also Figure 2.1), Reagan performed one of his most dramatic gestures. In response to a nationwide strike by federally employed air traffic controllers, he ordered that all 11,345 strikers be fired immediately and moved quickly to fill the strikers' jobs with replacement workers who had crossed union

RONALD REAGAN

October 20, 1980

Robert E. Poli, President
Professional Air Traffic Controllers
   Organization
444 Capitol Street
Washington, D. C.

Dear Mr. Poli:

I have been thoroughly briefed by members of my staff as to the deplorable state of our nation's air traffic control system. They have told me that too few people working unreasonable hours with obsolete equipment has placed the nation's air travellers in unwarranted danger. In an area so clearly related to public safety the Carter administration has failed to act responsibly.

You can rest assured that if I am elected President, I will take whatever steps are necessary to provide our air traffic controllers with the most modern equipment available and to adjust staff levels and work days so that they are commensurate with achieving a maximum degree of public safety.

As in all other areas of the federal government where the President has the power of appointment, I fully intend to appoint highly qualified individuals who can work harmoniously with the Congress and the employees of the government agencies they oversee.

I pledge to you that my administration will work very closely with you to bring about a spirit of cooperation between the President and the air traffic controllers. Such harmony can and must exist if we are to restore the people's confidence in their government,

Sincerely,

Ronald Reagan

RONALD REAGAN

901 South Highland Street, Arlington, Virginia 22204
Paid for by Reagan Bush Committee, United States Senator Paul Laxalt, Chairman. Ray Buchanan, Treasurer

Figure 2.1. *Reprint of Letter from Ronald Reagan to President of PATCO.*

picket lines. He then proceeded to have the union "decertified" as the legal bargaining agent.[47] It was a dramatic act against an innocuous and politically conservative craft union that had actually been one of the few unions to endorse Reagan's candidacy in the election, and whose utter desperation caused by the highly stressful working conditions in understaffed airport control towers had led it to an uncharacteristic violation of the law.[48]

It was a debacle. The head of the AFL-CIO made a symbolic show of joining the PATCO strikers on the picket line, and threats to shut down the nation's air system were loudly issued by union leaders representing various groups of airline workers, but substantive expressions of solidarity never materialized. It was a conspicuous public humiliation for the trade union movement, one that displayed the degree of economic violence that could be unleashed by a state willing, once again, as it had been in pre-1930s America, to shed any pretense of neutrality, while serving as an unequivocal encouragement to an assault on unions in the private sector.

Although preparations had been underway for well over a decade and the groundwork had certainly been laid in the concessions that had been wrung from labor, the employers' campaign against unionism was astonishing in its ferocity.[49] Its most evocative expression was manifested in the reemergence of strikebreaking as a systematic strategy of labor relations.[50] Official union-sanctioned strikes, which had been so thoroughly tamed by the whip of the Taft-Hartley Act three decades earlier, were now viewed by employers as an opportunity to relieve themselves of the burden of unionism, thus becoming a routine object of provocation. The formula was a simple four-step process:

1. "Bargain to Impasse": In the collective-bargaining process employers would limit negotiations to the most trivial issues (refusing to address those issues most important to the union) or would present the union with a list of contract concessions that would be untenable for the union to accept.

2. "Provoke a Strike": At the arrival of the contract expiration date the employer would refuse to compromise, forcing the union to either yield to all of their (untenable) demands or to strike. In many cases, workers angered by the inflexibility of their employer would strongly favor a strike in order to preserve a measure of collective self-respect.

3. "Hire 'Replacement Workers' ": With the strike underway, the employer would hire permanent-replacement workers (strikebreakers) to take the jobs of the strikers, thus maintaining production levels and removing any incentive or pressure on the employer to settle the conflict.[51]

4. "Break the Strike" (and the union): The replacement workers would be "discretely encouraged" to petition for a government-supervised decertification election. Once the strike was one full year old, only the *replacements* would be eligible to vote to nullify the legal standing of the union in that workplace or company.

Although the precise number of such strikes is unknown, with some important exceptions they tended to occur in small rather than large corporations, with plants located in a single community or region, rather than nationwide. A study of strikes that occurred in 1985 and 1989 indicated that permanent replacements were hired in one-third of all strikes, and that the *threat* of replacement workers was employed in many others.[52]

By the mid 1980s a new, multibillion-dollar industry had been established, offering legal advice, teams of management consultants, private security services, seminars, and manuals devoted to the new management problem of "union avoidance."[53] Throughout this period their work yielded an enormous trail of violence and social disruption, as thousands of union workers in hundreds of communities across the country found themselves embroiled in protracted and desperate "fights to the finish," for which they had been ill-prepared by the culture of business unionism. Communities were forced to defend unionism because their jobs and livelihoods depended on it. The irony is that in their defense of unionism they often created a unionism that was worth defending! In strike after strike (by copper miners in Arizona, coal miners in Virginia, paper workers in Maine and Wisconsin, food-processing workers in California, Iowa, and Minnesota, newspaper workers in New York and Detroit, and bus drivers and airline workers across the nation, strikes for which systematic analyses are available) solidarity and militancy were the absolute defining characteristics, particularly once replacement workers were hired and any possibility of collective retreat was foreclosed.[54]

The statistical data that exist indicate the extent of the losses suffered by labor, but a key problem in attempting to statistically represent the employer assault is that statistical representation itself can be seen to have been wielded as a weapon. That is, between 1979 and 1982, in the midst of the employer offensive, the Bureau of Labor Statistics (BLS) significantly curtailed its statistical coverage of strikes. Among other things, this meant that no

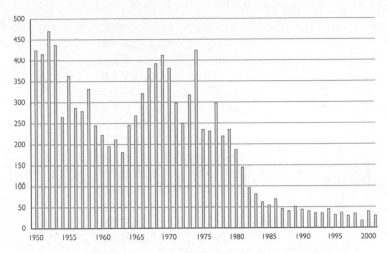

Figure 2.2. *U.S. Strikes and Lockouts, 1950–2000.* Source: United States Department of Labor, Bureau of Labor Statistics, "Work Stoppages Involving 1,000 Workers or More," (http://www.bls.gov).

longer would statistics be collected on such phenomena as small or medium-sized strikes, or strikes occurring "during term of agreement" (which, because more than 90 percent of union agreements contained a no-strike clause for the duration of the agreement, once provided a rough, but reasonably systematic estimate of the number of wildcat strikes). What was left of strike coverage was a single measure for large strikes and lockouts "involving 1,000 workers or more and lasting more than a single eight-hour shift." The yearly number of such strikes dropped precipitously as the employer offensive developed (see Figure 2.2). The number of decertification elections rose steadily as part of the union-busting campaign, averaging more than eight hundred per year during the height, which was four

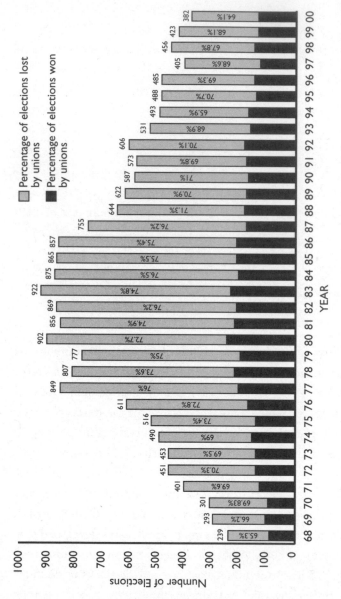

Figure 2.3. *Decertification Elections in the U.S., 1968–2000.* Source: Annual Reports of the National Labor Relations Board.

times the annual figure at the outset of the employer offensive (see Figure 2.3).

A systematic prevention strategy that has sought to close off the option of unionism to nonunion workers is an important part of the employer offensive that has continued to the present. Unsurprisingly, employers have benefited from a procedure that they have shaped, namely, that the negligible penalties for illegally firing and intimidating prounion employees during union-organizing drives makes it a very good investment. The result is that there have been tens of thousands of union activists fired annually, along with a sharp rise in the number of general "Unfair Labor Practice" charges against employers for illegally obstructing the union-representation process (see Figure 2.4).[55]

Despite the illegal activity, it was not at all necessary for employers to transgress the law in every instance. There is an extremely wide scope of activity that, while remaining within the letter of the law, effectively permits employers to deny union representation to workers.[56] For example, antiunion consultants are fully aware that the longer union elections are delayed, the more time there is for management to influence election outcomes through threats, promises, sudden wage increases, surveillance, as well as the hiring of new employees who have been carefully screened for any prounion predilections.[57] Furthermore, even when union-representation elections are successful, the NLRB may take several years before issuing an official bargaining order, thus giving employers a large window within which they are able to winnow the ranks of the union-organizing committee, dissipating the prounion sentiments of the workforce.

Moreover, a more subtle approach was for firms to maintain some of their operations in unionized workplaces while simulta-

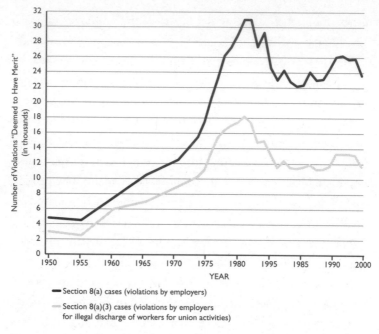

Figure 2.4. *Unfair Labor Practice Violations by Employers, 1950–2000.*
Source: Annual Reports of the National Labor Relations Board.

neously moving increasing amounts of investment to plants with no union representation, within the same company, often in "right-to-work" states. The scale of movement to such states in the 1980s alone was staggering, as unionized states in the North and Midwest lost 1.5 million manufacturing jobs and $40 billion in pay, many to the "right-to-work" states. The policy persists today; managers continue to rely on an informal policy, which directs them to always expand nonunion plants, never unionized ones. The result, over time, is that nonunion production sites into which investment has been channeled have begun to offer a significant technological edge over the increasingly obsolescent unionized units, which, along with their lower wages and benefits, further undermined the unionized plants.[58]

For unions, the result of the employer's assault was devastating: by 1995 union density in the private sector stood at barely 10 percent, lower than it had been even before the passage of the Wagner Act in 1935. And in absolute numbers, union membership dropped by almost 4 million workers between 1978 and 1995. The drop was especially precipitous among the ambitious industrial unions that had been so prominent in remaking the labor movement in the 1930s and 1940s. The United Automobile Workers, which epitomized the CIO in the minds of many, shrank from its postwar high of 1.4 million members to 751,000 in 1995. The United Steelworkers of America, which once held sway over the core of the American economy, suffered even greater losses, from a peak of 1,069,900 members to 403,000 members in 1995. And the United Mine Workers, whose leader, John L. Lewis, played such a crucial role in establishing the CIO and labor's upsurge in leading the New Deal, was by the 1990s only a diminished fragment of its former self.[59]

Why should American employers have been so much more aggressive in fighting unions than their Western European counterparts when both faced similar economic pressures? One major reason is that the institutional context—and hence the logic of profitability—is very different in Europe than it is in the United States. In Europe, the postwar system of social provision has been a *public* system, created through legislation and financed by *all* employers and taxpayers. Moreover, collective bargaining is centralized, with collective agreements routinely extended to nonunion workers in the same industry. European employers thus have much less to gain from breaking unions or fighting union-organizing drives than do American employers. In the United States, firm-centered bargaining, combined with a private system of social provision (covering only workers in unionized firms), together yield great financial rewards for those employers who can prevent the creation of a new union or get rid of the existing one.

In addition, unparalleled institutional opportunities for opposing unions were created by Taft-Hartley and honed to perfection in the years that followed. Even if European employers were equally hostile to unions, they would have few legal weapons for resisting them.

AT THE EDGE OF THE PRECIPICE

By all accounts, American labor has been on the ropes, reeling from the blows of an employer assault that has lasted more than two long decades. At the beginning of the twenty-first century union membership in the private sector had fallen to 9 percent of the labor force.[60] Although the employers' goal of a "union-free environment" has not yet been completely achieved, there has been a significant and unmistakable redistribution of both wealth (upward) and of working-class institutional power (downward) in American society, with the decline of the union movement representing both cause and effect.

The terrible irony is that the kind of oppositional stance and militant solidarity that would have been required to counter or even to slow the decline was traded away decades ago. Like a Faustian bargain, the employers returned to collect their due from a labor movement that had sold its soul by accepting the terms of the social contract. In sharp contrast to the radicals who built the CIO, the postwar generation of American labor leaders were schooled in the relentless pragmatism of the social contract, actively discouraging rank-and-file initiative and class solidarity as threats to the ordered, bureaucratic machinery of the grievance process and the labor board (to which, as the price of admission, they had been obliged to swear allegiance). This meant that for half a century, under the shroud of Taft-Hartley and subsequent legislation, the trade unions left largely uncultivated the solidarity of many millions of workers, allowing massive institutional resources to be squandered by refusing to invest in the very source of labor's strength, the culture of solidarity that had brought them into being in the first place.

At the edge of the precipice, pondering their own mortality, the labor bureaucrats fell silent. Yet it is precisely this vacuum that has afforded space for the emergence of new social forces and a new form of politics in the labor movement, tendencies that hold a fair measure of potential and that therefore embody a good deal of hope.

CHAPTER THREE

Bureaucrats, "Strongmen," Militants, and Intellectuals

"TEAMSTERS AND TURTLES — TOGETHER AT LAST!" read the hand-painted sign that bobbed up and down amid bodies and banners filling the streets of downtown Seattle. Everyone, it seems, saw that sign—not only those protesting in late November 1999, but also the millions watching the events on television. Because unionized truck drivers ("Teamsters") and environmental activists ("Turtles") are completely oxymoronic in American sociocultural terms, the slogan resonated singularly amid the tear gas, the barking chants, and the overall failure of the meeting itself (in the *New York Times* the Seattle World Trade Organization (WTO) meeting was variously termed "a collapse," "a shipwreck," "an embarrassment," and "a stinging blow" to U.S. trade initiatives). The picture of working-class trade unionists marching alongside and inhabiting the same social universe as middle-class environmental activists would not be surprising in Europe, but the image has been virtually unimaginable in the United States since midcentury, when the absence of a discernable "red" movement made even the suggestion of a "red/green alliance" into a thoroughly unnatural state of political affairs. Indeed, most Americans of a certain age maintain an image of workers in relation to Left political protest *not* as participants at all, but as counterprotesters, an impression that was firmly planted in the public imagination in 1970 when hundreds of New York City construction workers severely beat anti–Vietnam War demonstrators as they marched toward Wall Street.

The presence in Seattle of steelworkers, aircraft workers, teamsters, and other trade union groups was significant, both socially and symbolically, but it also needs to be understood in relation to the contradictory fact that only days prior to the demonstrations, John Sweeney, the president of the AFL-CIO, had actually joined with business leaders in endorsing President Clinton's trade agenda.[1] Thus while many union militants, including staff organizers dispatched from AFL-CIO headquarters, were openly mobilizing to protest against the WTO, the top union leadership was publicly giving its approval to it. To be sure, this was a realpolitik born of the precarious structural position of labor in American society, a continually humiliating posture in which the labor leadership is forced to cling to the Democratic Party, which is increasingly dominated by social forces who openly champion neoliberal reform and who mostly treat unions like unwanted relatives (while simultaneously relying on their electoral and financial support).

Although there is a process of change underway that holds the very real potential to be both significant and lasting, American labor remains ambivalent about accepting the role of an oppositional social movement. This hesitancy is due to a combination of factors, including the relatively limited influence of the reform leadership within a decentralized trade union structure, one that has been dominated by exceedingly cautious and bureaucratic labor organizations. In some respects the ambivalence simply re-iterates the contradictory tensions within the U.S. labor move-ment described earlier. In other, more significant ways, however, it can be seen to represent a very new situation in which the labor movement is caught moving in two directions at once, unable to reconcile the opposing historical trajectories because the institu-tional relationships in which they were formerly contained have now come apart. Our goal is to outline the social logic of this dy-namic, by sketching a view of the key social actors, both institu-tional and individual, who animate it.

In order to fully comprehend the social "impossibility" of Teamsters and Turtles together in Seattle, one must understand not only the powerful constraints imposed on postwar American labor by employers and the state but, just as importantly, the power of the *self*-imposed limits that are the product of changes within American trade unions themselves. That is, a bureau-cratic regime was actively foisted on American unions by a series of social and legal practices promoted by employers and their political supporters. This was a key part of a broad postwar pro-gram of socioeconomic pacification that involved the massive mobilization of political and judicial resources, including the in-corporation of "responsible" labor leaders and the broad cam-paign of de-radicalization and cultural purification that we call "McCarthyism." It also included passage of the Taft-Hartley Act, which de-fanged the movement and forced its leaders to be-come disciplinarians over the membership. This was not a sim-ple matter of an organizational "iron law," or an inexorable bu-reaucratic imperative, nor was it solely a matter of corporate domination. For although it was an unequivocal social victory for employers, it also represented a two-sided Faustian bargain through which a substantial segment of the labor leadership was willing to trade away a legacy of militant solidarity and radical political language in exchange for a measure of social legitimacy and institutional standing.

The postwar bureaucratization of the labor relations system did not simply occur coincidentally with the de-radicalization of the labor movement; it was partly facilitated by it. In other words, the anticommunist purge removed radicals from the shop floor and the union hall and expelled militant organizations from the "official" union movement. By removing many of those who viewed the workplace as a battleground (while putting on notice those who remained) it was that much easier to effectively supplant shop-floor militancy with a bureaucratic system of rule governance and judicial regulation. Furthermore, the context of rapid postwar economic expansion ensured a degree of compliance that would have been impossible to imagine in the midst of Depression-era conditions only a decade earlier. The point is that what occurred was a reciprocally confirming process by which most of the labor leadership acceded to a postwar regime that produced a distinctive variety of unionism, which, in turn and over time, also generated a distinctive type of union leader.[2]

THE BUREAUCRATIC PERSONALITY OF AMERICAN UNIONISM

The process of bureaucratization is, simultaneously, an act of institutionalization. As such, the postwar process of bureaucratization of labor relations served to provide the labor movement with a measure of institutional security. For a union movement whose survival, historically, had never been at all assured, any degree of institutional security seemed appealing, especially since it only required acceptance of an informal social contract that assured labor's place as a "junior partner" in the postwar order.

Generally speaking, bureaucratic forms of organization represent *extensions* of existing social relationships, inasmuch as they express, in organizational terms, the prevailing relations of dominance and subordination. In this way, bureaucratic forms of labor relations can be seen to reflect the institutional dominance of corporate interests. On another level, however, they can be seen as practices that have a capacity to *transform*, to the extent that bureaucratic practices create a new kind of social relationship. For example, when the industrial relations system established an orderly means of resolving disputes through a system of codified grievance procedures, the element of surprise was eliminated, or greatly reduced, thus producing a potentially significant shift in the balance of forces among the social actors in that relationship.[3] That is, bureaucracy had the effect of *altering* the nature of the social relationship by regularizing, rewarding, and otherwise providing support and sustenance, at an institutional level and over time, for certain kinds of actors and actions over other kinds. Thus, within the trade union structure, deal-makers, office managers, functionaries, and lawyers increasingly occupied the stage, pushing aside militants and rank-and-file workers who may have helped bring a union into being, while paperwork, the art of interpreting contractual language, and an adeptness at wielding procedural rules (codified by Robert's Rules of Order) were the sorts of skills and activities that became increasingly favored and seemingly more useful than the skills necessary for organizing workers, devising militant tactics, and galvanizing others.

In the United States the kind of unionism that prevailed throughout the postwar period has sometimes been termed "push-button unionism," with reference to the overly ordered character of labor relations, in contrast to the more wide-open conflict that was seen in earlier decades. Such reforms as the automatic dues "checkoff" system were emblematic, and though it appeared quite simple, its ramifications were profound. In those establishments where a union was authorized to bargain on behalf of the workers, the employer was legally mandated to regularly and automatically deduct the union membership dues from each employee's weekly paycheck and transfer that money to the headquarters of the trade union. On one level, this represented little more than an administrative courtesy. Unions were saved from having to collect weekly or monthly dues from tens of thousands of their members who were spread across the country in countless workplaces, large and small. It was of enormous practical help to trade union leaders, as well, because it assured a steady flow of income to the administration of the union bureaucracy and helped to regularize union membership lists. Furthermore, it was a public demonstration that employers had accepted the unions, a tangible expression of the social contract between business and labor.

But the institution of the automatic dues checkoff also meant that neither national nor local union leaders had to be in direct or regular contact with workers to ensure regular dues contributions, thereby contributing to a growing distance between the leadership and the rank and file. It also meant that the financial sustenance of the union no longer depended on cultivating principles of solidarity and trade unionism among the membership. Because the financial integrity of the organization no longer required a perpetual situation of worker mobilization, the mobilizing apparatus of most unions tended to enter a state of atrophy. In its place grew a union staff that was committed to dealing with work-site problems *for* workers rather than *with* workers. The mentality was one of "servicing" in which members had their dues deducted in exchange for a staff that would handle their grievances.

There were changes in the kinds of people who occupied staff positions in the unions as a result of such reforms. For example, in many, if not most industrial unions the position of the organizer, whose role was to be on the front lines, mobilizing workers against the employers and the forces of state repression, was increasingly giving way to the position of the business agent, whose job was much less concerned with the mobilization of workers than it was to the servicing of existing labor agreements. While the historic figure of the organizer has been symbolically woven into the lore of the class struggle, the job of the business agent is mostly absorbed by the minutiae of job specifications and the arcane language of the legal contract. Based in the craft union tradition, the business agent was essentially a work contractor who, within the building-trades unions, was responsible for supplying skilled labor to construction firms, while simultaneously limiting that supply "to preserve the privilege of union membership for a relative handful of favored men."[4] Whereas the calling of the organizer is to "organize the unorganized," the outlook of the business agent is one of pragmatism and insularity, two characteristics that exemplified the "official" postwar labor movement as a whole.

If union leaders had indeed become "managers of discontent," as some critics had designated them, then it was at least partly because the bureaucratic regulations governing postwar labor relations provided little alternative. Take the matter of grievances, for example. The standard system of grievance resolution inserted into most labor/management agreements was specifically designed to channel discontent away from the "heat" of the shop floor. No longer were workers meant to respond to injustice in the workplace by taking matters into their own collective hands. Instead, they were to register their complaint by initiating a legalistic procedure. Through it a union representative would be summoned to fill out a form on behalf of an individual worker, indicating the reasons why a specific grievance seemed to represent a violation of the specific terms of the contract. The union representative then filed the grievance form with the company and waited for a meeting to be scheduled with a company manager. If the grievance could not be resolved at the initial level, then it would continue upward through a series of "steps" to higher levels of union and management that would seek resolution, until, remaining unresolved, it would be submitted to neutral arbitration (in the form of a "mediation service," an enterprise that exists for the purpose of mediating industrial disputes). The important point is that this is a system of procedures that removes the resolution of injustice from its source, spatially, temporally, and socially, while designating functionaries as the primary actors in a social drama that has been drained of all dramatic content.

In contrast to an earlier generation of labor leaders who had been formed in and by the class warfare of the 1930s, the cohort of leaders who came of age in the postwar decades was largely shaped by practices of deal making, bureaucratic wrangling, and institutional administration. It was not only a matter of labor relations being increasingly governed bureaucratically, but also the unions themselves having become massive bureaucratic organizations with huge financial resources, that employed many layers of specialized staff, organized in various subdivisions. A good part of the reason for large union bureaucracies has to do with the fact that these unions administered their own systems of social provision. By contrast, in European societies, these tasks were coordinated at the national level by centralized government agencies.[5] By 1970 some 20 million American workers belonged to trade unions, with membership in several unions reaching more than 1 million (a result of the push-button unionism and the social compact on which it was based). The International Brotherhood of Teamsters with more than 2 million members, the United Automobile Workers with 1.35 million members, the United Steelworkers with 1.2 million members, the International Union of Electrical Workers with 980,000 members, and the International Association of Machinists with 900,000 members were the largest unions.[6] These were organizations with annual revenues in the tens of millions of dollars, presided over by leaders charged with overseeing huge investment portfolios. In certain respects, the union leader maintained a professional profile that would have been hard to distinguish from his counterpart at the negotiating table, the corporate president (who may also have been his golfing partner).

Those union organizations that grew to be large and powerful in the postwar decades tended to be those in the industries that held dominant positions in the U.S. economy (for example, the automobile, steel, and electronics industries) or which represented workers occupying critical nodes in the economy (like coal miners and truck drivers). While in organizational terms these unions represented an industrial unionism that was not so very different from that which had been formed by the CIO, it was an industrial unionism *with the radicalism removed.* In other words it was a domesticated industrial unionism whose institutional standing was made relatively secure. Moreover, it had eschewed the language and the practice of a radicalism that had previously been the foundation for mass mobilization, for an activated membership, and for a unionism where much of the initiative had flowed in an upward direction.

The process of habituation to this more bureaucratic form of unionism was partly facilitated by the simple fact that postwar labor leaders tended to be older men than in previous generations, to hold their terms in office for longer periods, and to work in unions in which leadership changes were less frequent than they had once been. For example, when comparing national leadership changes in the early decades of the twentieth century to those in the 1960s, one observes an average of 1.75 changes in top union leadership at the beginning of the twentieth century, but only .57 changes between 1960 and 1970.[7] Studies of national, state, and local labor leaders conducted in 1946 and 1976 indicated that leaders in the latter study tended to be older, to have gained their union office at an older age, to have been a union member for a longer period, and to have been in the labor movement for a longer period before gaining union office than the earlier (1946) generation (many of whom had entered office in the upheavals of the 1930s) (see Table 3.1). In other words, a more heavily bureaucratic postwar unionism was partly brought about by leaders who were older than their predecessors and had

Table 3.1. *Characteristics of Top Union Leaders,*
1946 and 1976[8]

	1946	1976
Age	45.9	53.7
Age when position acquired	40.6	44.6
# of years in labor movement	16.7	27.8
# of years in labor movement prior to acquiring position	11.5	18.9

served longer in union office, factors that helped facilitate the process of their habituation to it.

"THE INVISIBLE MAN" AND "THE SULTAN"

The range of leadership types produced in the postwar labor movement has been rather narrow because the personal styles of union leaders have tended to conform, more or less, to the organizational personalities of their unions. Obviously this is in addition to the specific characteristics of an individual's career trajectory, including the general occupational culture of the industry out of which one might have emerged, the "cohort effect" of the historical period in which one joined the labor movement, as well as the actual circumstances by which one attained his or her leadership position. But once these differences are taken into account, it can be said fairly that, for the most part, above the level of the shop floor, the American labor movement has not produced many bold or imaginative leaders, nor has the American labor leader had very much of a distinctive persona or public presence in the society. In fact, apart from a very small handful of personalities whose images became more or less known to the general public from their occasional appearances in the visual media, the average postwar American labor leader has been an "invisible man."[9]

A state of invisibility can be seen, in part, as a stylistic reflection of the bureaucratic structure of labor organizations. That is, the seemingly styleless leadership was basically labor's equivalent of the "Organization Man," the bureaucrat with the "bureaucratic personality" whose distinctive character was a determined lack of distinctiveness.[10] The relationship between organizational and individual personality is more complicated than a basic correspondence, and in the case of the labor leadership, the relationship was not a politically neutral one. That is, the stylelessness of the postwar labor leader can be seen as having been symbolically significant as a negative political assertion, a stylistic representation of what he was *not*. He was certainly not the picture of the charismatic revolutionary that might have been readily associated with radicals of the 1930s or with labor militants most everywhere else in the world, but tended to affirm a near colorless public persona that resembled more the clerk than the social rebel (see sidebar, page 91).

This was clearly not a self-presentation intended to create a strong association with the worker. The postwar labor leader did not dress in workman's clothing, even though he might have carried himself in a body type that betrayed his working-class origins (and that sometimes made his clothing seem rather ill fitting) and was much more likely to resemble somebody in sales or in small business, rather than a union militant. The very picture of "responsibility," the leaders of American trade unions represented themselves as safe and predictable, and above all, *not* as communists or rebels of any sort.

Ironically, it was colorlessness that was perhaps the most striking characteristic of Lane Kirkland, who, as president of the AFL-
CIO from 1979 to 1995, served as the public face of the labor
movement during the steepest part of its institutional decline.
Kirkland, whose own experience as an active union member had
been confined to a brief stint as a chief mate aboard a merchant
marine vessel during the Second World War, was the perfect bureaucrat who had been handpicked to be president by his prede-
cessor, George Meany, after a twenty-year career as Meany's chief
minion within the organization.[11] When he emerged from of the
dim corridors of the AFL-CIO bureaucracy to take over as president, Kirkland was largely unknown, not only to the American
public but to most union members. Thus the public face of
American labor was a perfectly faceless bureaucrat. Even more
significantly, when he stepped down from his position as president
of the federation in 1995, Kirkland was probably not much more
widely known than he had been when he stepped into the position
sixteen years earlier.

Kirkland displayed a blandness of personality that was characteristic of American trade union leaders, most of whom had spent
the bulk of their careers acting as office managers rather than as
militants. But while invisibility was the modal type of persona produced by postwar American unionism, there were organizational
configurations that produced a different, distinctly authoritarian
strain of leadership as well. With authoritarian leaders, organizations can appear as reflections, or as extensions of their peculiar
personal style. Thus "big men" like John L. Lewis and later Tony
Boyle of the United Mine Workers of America (UMWA), Jimmy
Hoffa of the Teamsters Union, and Joseph Ryan of the International Longshoremen's Association, all infamous for their

"NOTORIETY DOESN'T EXCITE ME THAT MUCH"

These reflections were offered by Marshal M. Hicks, a former power-company worker who, at the time of this interview in 1989, was secretary-treasurer of the Utility Workers Union of America, a small national union of 46,000 workers, most of whom are employed by private and public electric utility companies, such as nuclear power plants, and water, gas, and sewage utility companies.

I was involved in organizing when I was regional director in the field, and while I really didn't mind it, I would say it's not my most enjoyable activity. First of all, I'm not the type of person who meets people easily. I'm kind of quiet and don't talk too much, so it's very difficult for me to just go up to a stranger whom I've never seen before and start a general discussion. I can talk business with anybody, but just to become pal-sy with somebody is not really part of my nature. But I did do it as part of the job.

I really enjoyed working on grievances because that's something where I can help someone directly and individually.

Looking back over all the things I've done in the union, I think the position I learned the most from was probably the time I was the vice-president/secretary-treasurer on the Michigan council. While I was there I got involved with the job evaluation process and learned to interpret duties and jobs and apply values to them. I also had the opportunity to present arbitration cases, and also cases before the NLRB [National Labor Relations Board] and the Unemployment Commission in Michigan

Notoriety doesn't excite me that much. Unions are born out of a necessity, and we don't need to do advertising, on television or anywhere else, to convince people that unions are necessary. I've never really believed you can sell a narrow viewpoint like ours by just blasting it on TV day in and day out.

I probably take a simplistic view, but if I can do a good job for somebody and accomplish something, even if the other guy's mad or not satisfied with what I've done, I'll be satisfied as long as I know I've done my best.

SOURCE: Quaglieri, *America's Labor Leaders*, ch. 13.

autocratic methods of leadership, were men whose personae were imprinted onto their organizations by a combination of strength of personality, ruthlessness, and "cronyism," methods that bear a striking resemblance to the characteristics of political "bosses" who reigned in a host of large American cities in the early decades of the twentieth century.

The phenomenon of the "strongman" has a long history in the American labor movement and has been reflected in the leaders' willingness and ability to systematically employ undemocratic and even coercive methods to maintain themselves in positions of power.[12] This was power more often deployed in the service of greed than ideological vision, with the practice of political leadership crafted to conceal and protect the corrupt practices. Too often, the union's treasury became the personal reserve of the "big man," like Edward Hanley, who served as president of the Hotel Employees and Restaurant Employees International Union (HERE) for twenty-five years until his forced retirement in 1998. He was a man without a cohesive or even identifiable political vision, and though frequently criticized for maintaining friendly relations with organized-crime families, his most egregious violations of union position were perhaps best summarized by one hotel worker and union member who noted, "He was very generous to himself with our money."[13] Besides a $2.5 million jet plane that the union had purchased for his personal use and the office that it rented for him near his Palm Springs, California, vacation home, on his "retirement" Hanley had been able to arrange to continue receiving an annual salary of $300,000 (for the rest of his life). This is *in addition* to the *three* pensions and an independent retirement account that had been established for him.[14]

Even in those unions that have maintained a reasonable degree of democratic practice at the national level, pockets of authoritarian rule can be sustained at a regional or local level. Until recently, an example of this sort of disjuncture was manifested in the Service Employees International Union (SEIU), John Sweeney's former union. In 1999 Gus Bevona was finally forced out as local president of SEIU's New York local, representing 55,000 building maintenance workers (janitors, doormen, and elevator operators). With an annual salary of $450,000, Bevona's extravagance had become an open embarrassment for a union that was at the forefront of reform efforts nationwide. The national union leadership placed the New York City local under an administrative trusteeship, thereby removing Bevona along with several of his cronies, but before departing he arranged to receive $1.5 million dollars in severance and unused vacation pay.[15] On his removal from office, Bevona was forced to relinquish what the *New York Times* described as a "palatial penthouse" above the union's New York City headquarters, which reportedly was built with "enough marble to empty a quarry" and that contained a wall of twelve television monitors behind a massive desk, a vantage point that he reportedly used "to spy on subordinates elsewhere in the building."[16] Bevona had maintained his position at the top of the New York local with the aid of a powerful political machine that consisted of highly paid business agents and local executive board members who ensured his reelection in exchange for their positions. The creation of a figure like Gus Bevona was possible in a union like SEIU because its tradition of local autonomy allowed for the accumulation of considerable power at the local level, conditions that permitted this kind of contemporary "sultanism" to flourish.[17]

Comparable conditions have been especially prevalent in the

building-trades unions where, historically, craft union power rested on monopoly control over local labor markets, a situation that afforded local union leaders considerable personal power in their relations with both construction employers who depended on skilled labor, and with the skilled tradesmen who depended on a union card for access to regular work. As one analyst has noted, "Through their control over union hiring halls and their collusive agreements with employers, many union officials, especially in the construction trades, use their control over job referrals to build their political machines and to starve out critics."[18] The local labor leader in the construction trades was basically a labor broker with the power to disrupt a construction job through his control over the supply of skilled labor. This power was partly masked by the familiarity of interpersonal relationships and a style of informality that is the product of having been a member of a "brotherhood" of journeymen in an overwhelmingly masculine occupational culture. In this world, where ritualized good-natured banter serves as a mark of belonging, it is in the interest of the union leader to maintain friendly, or at least familiar interpersonal relationships to facilitate the periodic tour of job sites (to calibrate the balance of labor supply and demand in the local construction labor market, where many small construction jobs may be underway at any given time). Furthermore, with only negligible differences of status and pay between skilled workers and construction foremen, the movement between ranks is often fluid, thus preserving familiar or casual interpersonal relations.[19] Habituation to such a form of unionism at the local level is not necessarily abandoned as one rises through the ranks of the union leadership (see sidebar, page 96).

In addition to a certain informality and familiarity at a stylistic level, there is a particular provincial outlook that has predominated in the building-trades unions, a provincialism that is produced in an industry whose activity is frequently administered at the local level by local public officials and functionaries, even when the private or public capital that supports it has originated from a more distant (state, federal, or corporate) source. Within such a framework, it has always been in the interest of the building-trades unions to cultivate a strong political and civic presence at the local (municipal) level of government, for it is there that state or federal construction projects have been managed and their contracts awarded. It is also for this reason that the building-trades unions, along with the narrow pragmatism of their craft union vision, have tended to be heavily represented on local central labor councils, thereby placing a particularly conservative stamp on the local public visage of trade unionism.[20]

On reaching the upper ranks of his organization, the building-trades union leader has often carried with him the methods by which he wielded power at the local level, therefore reproducing at a regional or national level a certain style of leadership within an arena where the resources and the stakes are considerably higher. Such leaders take on the resemblance of the feudal chieftain, ringed by loyal retainers, and because the most trusted of whom may be immediate family members, the "family dynasty," or at least its appearance, has not been uncommon in American unionism.[21]

Let's not forget that these various styles of leadership only make sense in relation to a style of unionism that consciously eschewed those characteristics that labor movements everywhere (including in the United States) once adopted by reflex, namely, the languages and the practices of class warfare, of solidarity, and of internationalism. The postwar versions of unionism in the

"A NONADVERSARIAL UNIONISM"

The following is an excerpt of the reflections of John S. Rogers, former general secretary of the United Brotherhood of Carpenters and Joiners of America from 1989.

Our role as a trade union movement is to serve as a lobby for the people. . . . The little guys rely upon us. We're the only labor movement in the world that embraces the social, political, and economic system of its country. Every other labor union or labor movement in the world fights to change the system. We only struggle here to humanize the system.

Here we are an organization in our 106th year as an international union and for fifty-five of those years a Hutcheson was at the helm — that's fifty-five consecutive years with William L., and then Maurice. Our membership is middle class, conservative by nature, and very conservative by trade union standards. But let me say that we have always been out front on social and justice matters. Our organization was out in the forefront, maybe not ideologically, but out there nevertheless, of the civil rights movement. Old man Hutcheson was the general president then, and he sent the word out, "We're not going to have black locals anymore, we're not going to have white locals anymore, we're going to have locals." And back in the thirties we said, "We don't go for this commie business," and we purged the commies.

(continued)

United States, whether of the narrow craft union variety or of the narrow bureaucratic-industrial union model, were historically fashioned to erase any trace of socialism. This was not only true in an ideological sense but in a practical, organizational sense as well, where the relentless pragmatism of business unionism and the bureaucratic regime to which it became adapted have served as a powerful counterweight. Apart from a very tiny handful of unions that remained outside of the fold, through the second half of the twentieth century most American unions can be seen to have been characterized by the following characteristics:[22]

(continued)

Others came to us and said, "How'd you do it?" Hutcheson said, "I just threw the bastards out!"

People on the management side and I have an excellent relationship. I have always maintained the greatest type of nonadversarial relationship with them that I could. I've always just felt that you could do better by keeping the lines open than shutting them down. In fact, for many years I was liaison with all of the management groups that we deal with around the country. I know them all, the Iacoccas, the General Motors people, the big utilities, the big construction corporations, and while we may not agree all the time, at least we sit down and listen. If we don't agree with one another, we'll tell the other fellow.

The scales though are definitely tipped in management's favor now. They have gotten real tough since the Reagan administration came in. We've got three major impasses right now on the West Coast with the three biggest guys in the lumber industry, Louisiana Pacific, Weyerhauser, and Georgia-Pacific. Our relationships with the employers in the construction industry though are very different; it's more of a partnership relationship. They're out competing in the marketplace, and oh, we have problems, but by and large, we're in a sinking ship together. If they don't get the jobs, our members don't work. So we work very closely with them.[23]

SOURCE: Quaglieri, *America's Labor Leaders*, ch. 23.

1. A strong reliance on the formal procedural requirements of the highly bureaucratized industrial relations system;

2. A strictly top-down hierarchical structure that discourages rank-and-file initiative;

3. Closed channels of communication networks at the top that rely on secretive "backroom" deals and create the conditions that produce an ill-informed and passive membership;

4. Democratic forms that often coexist with undemocratic practices;

5. A unionism that reacts to employer initiatives, rather than acting proactively;

6. Aggressive antiradicalism, frequently employed to contain internal political opposition; and

7. An active opposition to labor militancy, except on rare occasions, and only when it can be tightly controlled by union staff.

A VOICE IN THE WILDERNESS

The reform leadership that came to power in the AFL-CIO in 1995 was headed by the triumvirate of John Sweeney, Richard Trumka, and Linda Chavez-Thompson, who together comprised an opposition slate in the first contested presidential election in the history of the federation.[24] It is essential to recognize the significance of the simple fact of a contested election. Prior to the delegate convention where the election occurred, it had been fully expected that Lane Kirkland would continue as president, or would simply anoint his successor, just as George Meany had anointed him. For forty years, from the 1955 merger of the AF of L and the CIO, the labor federation had only been headed by these two reactionary cold warriors, men who presided over an organization that tolerated very little internal dissent. In 1995 Kirkland, the personification of the unimaginative "organization man," was forced to accept an electoral challenge whose occurrence was no less surprising than its outcome.[25]

The "palace coup" that resulted from this first-ever electoral contest can be seen to have been a product of several related factors. First, the sheer power of the employer assault on unionism meant that those labor leaders who still adhered to the implicit "social contract" between business and labor were utterly bereft of answers as they were forced to see that many employers were no longer prepared to recognize the existence of unions. The sense of bewilderment felt as that realization began to set in was reflected in the comments of John Serembus, president of a small trade union that represented workers in the furniture and casket-making industries (which has since merged with the steelworkers' union), who remarked in the mid-1980s:[26]

> I think that we're fast approaching a return to the era of the
> 1920's and the 1930's, when people desperately fought for
> their right to have unions. . . . What's happened? Well, we
> now have a president [Reagan] in the White House, who
> is anti-labor, and with your right-to-work groups we're fast
> getting back to that era. In fact, it's the first time in my life-
> time I've seen police dogs, security guards with clubs and
> guns and surveillance equipment out at the picket lines,
> and I've been active as a member for forty-three years.
> I've seen these things in only the last three or four years.
> When Ronald Reagan was elected in 1980, I thought that
> was the best thing that could happen to the union move-
> ment. I said, "This can't be happening. He'll be out of there
> in four years, and he'll make people realize why they need
> unions." Well, he got a second term and just decimated
> our ranks. . . . Maybe it's too much for me to comprehend,
> I don't know.

A decade later, by 1995, many such union leaders felt they had little to lose by breaking with traditional etiquette to support an electoral challenge to the old regime. The challenge was spearheaded by Gerald McEntee, president of the American Federation of State, County, and Municipal Employees (AFSCME), at the time the second-largest trade union in the federation, with 1.2 million members, and by John Sweeney, who headed SEIU, the third-largest union. Because SEIU was one of the very few national unions whose membership had been growing in the 1990s, Sweeney could legitimately claim to offer a real alternative to the delegates of a movement that seemed to be hurtling rapidly into oblivion. But why had SEIU been able to grow in a period when so many other unions could not?

In addition to an aggressive merger strategy that has brought smaller unions into its fold, SEIU had been able to grow throughout the postwar decades by expanding beyond its original base in building services. SEIU had actively organized clerical workers, health care workers, and state and local government employees, a situation that permitted SEIU to ride the wave of public-sector expansion in the 1960s and 1970s as well as the massive growth of the health care sector in the decades since. While fierce employer opposition was battering unionism throughout the private sector, from the mid-1970s onward, the situation has been less difficult for unions in the public sector, where employers have less incentive, interest, or ability to openly mount aggressive campaigns to prevent or oust unions, since public officials are subject to political pressures. Moreover, the inherently political nature of public-sector unionism has made it possible to amend state labor laws to bring a version of push-button unionism to the public sector at the same time as unionism has been largely foreclosed in the private sector.[27]

While the membership of most other unions was being steadily eroded in the face of the Reagan-era employer offensive, and while resources for organizing new members remained miniscule in so many unions that had grown complacent from the push-button unionism of the postwar social contract, John Sweeney had doubled the union dues of SEIU members to support an increase in the staff of the national union (the size of the staff of this traditionally decentralized union reportedly grew from twenty to two hundred between 1984 and 1988).[28] Many of the new staff members were organizers who had been activists in various social movements of the 1960s and 1970s, and they brought aggressive and innovative organizing techniques to SEIU as it began to mobilize new members across an expanding service sector.

SEIU was an organization that was more structurally open to innovation than other unions. With its history as an AFL craft union, SEIU had been a highly decentralized organization with a strong tradition of local autonomy, structured more as a loose configuration of local urban fiefdoms than as a national union organization. This is precisely the kind of situation that could produce the "sultanism" of a Gus Bevona in the New York City local and that produced autocratic leaders in many of the building-trades unions. But whereas most traditional AFL craft unions tended to be organizations of highly skilled workers (like the building trades) the roots of SEIU were as a union of building service workers and were therefore much less "aristocratic," with members who enjoyed few of the craftsman's privileges. According to Michael Piore, much like some of the other unions associated with unskilled trades, such as those in the laundry industry or the hotel and restaurant industry, SEIU is a union whose decentralization has not only tended to accommodate corrupt local union officials (like Gus Bevona), but has also permitted "radical labor leaders and innovative organizational experiments that other unions would have been quick to stifle or expel."[29] SEIU was thus historically susceptible to the very sorts of reforms advanced by John Sweeney that encouraged both a strong measure of creativity in organizing and for hiring radicals as organizers.

The membership growth of SEIU provided Sweeney with the legitimacy to mobilize the presidents of twenty other unions at the 1995 AFL-CIO convention (who together represented 56 percent of the thirteen million votes of the federation) to oppose Lane Kirkland, and then when he stepped down, to defeat Thomas Donahue, the designated heir to the throne.[30] These twenty-one unions essentially represented what amounted to an informal and mildly social democratic "bloc" within the eighty-member (now sixty-five member) labor federation. Among the most prominent of their number, they included Ron Carey, the (former) reform president of the Teamsters, Richard Trumka of the Mine Workers, George Kourpias of the Machinists Union, Owen Bieber of the Automobile Workers, George Becker of the Steelworkers, Frank J. Hanley of the Operating Engineers, Sigurd Lucasson of the Carpenters Union, along with McEntee of AFSCME and Sweeney of SEIU.[31]

An often unnoticed, but not insignificant factor involved in the successful electoral challenge to the old regime had to do with the place and the position of the "outsiders" within American unions. Union leaders in the postwar decades became proficient in the exercise of internal control over dissidents in their unions. This skill was a necessity, since an often-unrecognized product of a narrow and overly bureaucratic business unionism is the militant and democratic opposition spawned in reaction and in relation to it. Vilified by union leaders and corporate management alike, the dissident groups that emerged in many American trade unions during the past half-century have served at least two important purposes. The first has been as a constant reminder of the undemocratic practices through which leadership regimes have been able to maintain themselves in power, and the second has been to periodically disrupt the social tranquility that such stability is meant to provide to employers. At certain times in certain organizations union reformers have been able to successfully overcome the seemingly overwhelming power of incumbency to win control of national unions or their local branches. Once in power, they have successfully shifted the priorities and the directional flow of union activity (see sidebar, page 104).

For example, a clear and demonstrable line of succession can be traced from the militant Miners for Democracy, a rank-and-file caucus formed in the late 1960s in opposition to a corrupt and undemocratic national leadership in the UMWA, through to the victory of Richard Trumka as president of the UMWA, and later to his accession to the second-highest position in the AFL-CIO itself. And the election of dissident reformer Ron Carey to the presidency of the Teamsters Union would have been impossible without the support of Teamsters for a Democratic Union, a militant group that had long fought against an entrenched leadership that was widely viewed in the labor movement as being too close to both corporate management and to networks of organized crime. Although short-lived, Carey's leadership of the huge Teamsters Union was significant for creating the mathematical opportunity for John Sweeney and his New Voice slate to garner enough delegate votes to win the AFL-CIO election in 1995.[32]

Other categories of "outsiders" have begun to achieve new status with the rise of the New Voice leadership, in-

"THE OUTSIDER WITHIN"

The following is an excerpt of reflections by Ed Mann (1928–92), a former militant rank-and-file leader of the United Steelworkers in Youngstown, Ohio. In 1973 Mann was elected president of the three-thousand-member Local 1462 in the Brier Hill mill, a position he held until the mill closed in 1979.

When I started at Brier Hill it was a big plant. . . . We had some strong young people with ideals. We believed in what the union was supposed to be like.

Before the local was organized, a lot of Italians lived in the vicinity of the plant. They were discriminated against as much as blacks were discriminated against. They got the lousiest jobs. They did track labor. They were helpers in the mason gang. They could not aspire to the jobs in the shops that the Germans or the English had. Most of the Italians were of limited formal education. They couldn't express themselves as well as those that they called "Johnny Bulls," the English, Irish, and Scots.

There was a young guy who was very literate named Danny Thomas. He was tough. If a foreman was mistreating an old Italian guy, he'd grab the foreman by the shirt and say, "Leave that old

(continued)

cluding women, non-White immigrants, and racial and ethnic minorities—categories of workers historically excluded and discriminated against in the structures of leadership of many trade unions. The election of Linda Chavez-Thompson from AFSCME to her position in the top leadership group has been viewed as a significant symbolic gesture in this regard, but even more significant have been the attention and resources devoted by unions like SEIU, HERE, District 1199 (a union of East Coast hospital workers, now a branch of SEIU), and the Union of Needletrades, Industrial and Textile Employees (UNITE, a

(continued)

guy alone!" So he got a lot of respect in the Italian community. Danny Thomas was president of Local 1462 from the late 1940s until the early 1960s, when he became a staff man for the international union. He was a real dictator as president. He made all kinds of deals.

We had the most dishonest elections you can imagine. One time they had a bottomless ballot box and they set it over a cold air return in the old house that we used as a union hall. As you voted you put your ballot in the box. It would drop down into the cellar. There were two people down there. "This one's OK." They'd put is aside. "This one's no good." They'd throw it in the furnace. (We heard this after these guys retired, years later.) . . . That was the game that was played. We learned early: if you don't have the power to count the votes, you don't have the power to win.

We knew we had two battles to fight, one with the company and one with the union. We weren't interested in breaking away or destroying the union. But we felt that the union had to be more responsive to what the members needed.

The union thought that what was good for the company was good for the union. I don't agree.

SOURCE: Lynd and Lynd, *New Rank and File*, pp. 98–99.

union of clothing-manufacturing workers) to aggressively organize among previously excluded and socially stigmatized groups.

Another important factor has been the fall of the Berlin Wall and the breakup of the Soviet Union, events that have made available a degree of ideological space in which the public display of "disloyalty" can be permitted, something that had been largely foreclosed during the cold war where anticommunism had served as a stick to beat back dissidents, Democrats, and militants in the labor movement. As the cold war has lifted, so has the basis for the compulsory self-censorship that has governed not only the labor movement but also many of the institutions of American society. With the ritualized incantation of anticommunism no longer required as ideological passkey for entrance to trade union circles, the labor movement has again become a place where social criticism can be expressed and even fostered.[33] At the same time, despite this very real leavening, the leadership of the American labor movement continues to be inhabited by men and women whose subjective horizons reflect the practical and institutional limitations imposed by a system of labor relations that has been overwhelmingly subordinated to corporate interests. In other words, the labor movement has opened up in significant ways, but not in all ways. American labor is still bound to the realities of a distinctly American configuration of social, ideological, and institutional power and to those practices permitted by that reality.

TOWARD A NEW "LABOR METAPHYSIC"

With the old AFL craft unions and the core industrial unions of the mass-production industries in decline, the changes at the top of the AFL-CIO have both reflected and facilitated the ascendance of unions whose memberships are concentrated in the public and service sectors of the economy. Although there are significant differences between and within them, unions such as SEIU, HERE, UNITE, AFSCME, the Communication Workers of America, and the higher-education division of the United Automobile Workers, are among the most dynamic unions in the labor movement.[34] But the real potential for change represented by the U.S. labor movement actually lies perhaps less in the growth and development of individual unions than it does in the development of the space *between* unions. This refers specifically to advances that are both symbolic and organizational, though we hasten to add that such distinctions tend to collapse in reality since organizational configurations not only have a practical utility (making new things happen) but also embody symbolic signification (making new meaning).

Generally speaking, analyses of the labor movement tend to focus on its corporeal dimensions (its size, its organizational structure, its institutional leverage, its membership characteristics, and so on) while disregarding or minimizing its evocative dimensions. However, the very strength and efficacy of the labor movement's embodied forms depends, to a considerable degree, on its capacity to invoke something larger than itself. In other words, a successful labor movement must have the capacity to rise above its corporeal or institutional form through a kind of sacred narrative, or myth, and solidarity has been a cornerstone of the foundational myth of labor movements everywhere. Solidarity represents a potent mythic theme that carries remarkably transcendent qualities. Under certain conditions and at certain moments, demonstrations of solidarity can summon powerful spiritual forces in the social world (in groups, in collective activities, and in organizational forms) that are capable of producing extraordinary degrees of selflessness and of collective identification. This is not a tautology, because by seeming to demonstrate the possibility of the impossible, dramatic displays of solidarity can encourage even broader and bolder practices of solidarism, and this is perhaps especially so in a society rife with social division and atomization.[35]

Demonstrated expressions of solidarity are capable of "charming" the social world by a process of symbolic levitation, in which even the most prosaic, mundane event (a meeting, a grievance, a contract negotiation) can quite suddenly rise to the level of the sacred. The singular voice thus turns into a collective chant, an individual's grievance is transformed into a collective protest, or a picket line is consecrated as the site of a powerful moral crusade. Although the expression "labor metaphysic" may have once been a term of derision, directed as a criticism of blind (left-wing) faith, it expresses quite reasonably an important dimension of collective action. Indeed, one measure of its truthfulness is the fact that an entire system of industrial bureaucracy was imposed in the United States precisely because of its incorporative power to domesticate, to channel, and to otherwise blunt the powerful social energies that might be released by practices of labor solidarity. So, when we say that one might look for change in the "space between unions" we partly mean through a reconfiguration of the place of the labor movement in the symbolic vocabulary of the society. But we also mean it in a literal sense as well, in terms of the development of several new organizational forms that are coming to occupy the spaces between existing unions, between unions and other institutions (communities and their organized representatives, social movements, religious organizations, and so on), and between the labor movement and those stigmatized social groups previously excluded or ignored by it.

One example is represented by the effort to revitalize the structure and practice of the six hundred central labor councils (CLCs) that exist across the United States. Central labor councils are local (city-, county-, or regionwide) federations of local unions and consist of the various trades and occupations represented in a local geographic area. In earlier periods, and most notably in the 1930s, central labor councils served as important institutional mechanisms for cultivating labor solidarity across industries and trades and for building interunion networks of leaders and organizations. Such bodies often served as the filament that tied together a wider community of labor, serving as the institutional vehicle through which solidarism was practiced and demonstrated, in-between those moments of intense crisis and struggle that would make it a vital necessity. Like the labor movement as a whole, the militancy of central labor councils waned and their purpose shifted in the decades of the postwar period. The most effective of them became political lobbying organizations that were active at the state level, but such efforts were never particularly effective, owing to a legislative program that was (and is) subordinated to an incorporated and increasingly conservative Democratic Party and to the lack of effective strategies for mobilizing the voting power of union members behind such a narrow program.[36] For the most part, central labor councils became largely ceremonial bodies dominated by local labor chieftains that served to ritualize the institutional status of trade unions through local charitable work, an activity that bound unions to the local businesses, fraternal orders, and civic associations that they had come to resemble in both style and ideology.

Although sporadic changes were well underway even earlier, the current AFL-CIO leadership has given a high priority to systematically changing the nation's central labor councils. In some areas, these changes have been substantial. In 1996, the federation organized a national conference of CLCs that provided workshops on methods for developing interunion and union-community networks, and a twenty-two member CLC advisory council was formed by John Sweeney to set priorities and direction for a reduced number of local labor councils. A serious discussion was initiated within the advisory council about the most effective ways to employ labor councils to facilitate union-organizing efforts, to assist unions in bargaining with employers, and to mobilize community support for workers' rights at the local level. Out of this debate emerged the "Union Cities" project, an initiative that is providing extra resources from the federation to those central labor councils willing and able to meet a specific set of goals, including:

1. A commitment to devote one-third of resources to organizing, by either assisting individual unions or by mounting multiunion organizing campaigns;
2. To implement a program of "Street Heat," or a local "rapid response" network to mobilize union members via telephone and e-mail to participate, on short notice, in demonstrations and other collective actions designed to pressure antiunion employers and public officials;
3. To pressure local governments to pass measures that support the right of workers to organize, as one means of creating a more favorable climate for organizing; and
4. To assure greater ethnic, racial, and gender representation in the work of central labor councils, in order to provide a public face for labor that more accurately reflects the social composition of the labor force itself.[37]

The Union Cities project represents a potentially significant revitalization of the central labor council idea. This project has created a geographically based institutional mechanism for multiunion cooperation, an organization embodying interunion solidarity at the local level that has largely been missing in American society for many decades. It has also put into place a framework for extending the labor movement beyond the bounds of the workplace, outward to the broader society.[38]

Developing linkages between union organizations and community groups is increasingly facilitated by forces that have emerged from within the labor movement, but that have existed in an oppositional tension to its dominant tendencies and official bodies. Previously the AFL-CIO leadership openly disdained protest movements of all kinds, and this included "Jobs with Justice," a national network of thirty locally based coalitions that had been created a decade ago by several national union leaders frustrated with labor's insularity. Consisting of union locals, neighborhood and community organizations, student, environmental, and women's groups who have made a commitment to join each other's picket lines and demonstrations, it is a grouping that has demonstrated a reasonably strong mobilizing presence in several large cities, including Atlanta, Boston, Cleveland, New York, and Seattle.[39]

Despite this resurgence of labor "leftism," many union leaders and members are distrustful, and even hostile to Left social activism, and the AFL-CIO leadership must continually operate in a way that avoids alienating them further by associating the labor movement too closely with social disruption. Still, the "Jobs with Justice" coalitions are able to count on the tacit support and encouragement of the national labor federation, and in certain local areas such coalitions work openly and easily alongside the official central labor council, sharing both resources and personnel. In the U.S. context, such interaction must be considered remarkable, given the troubled history of unions and the Left.

The development of so-called workers' centers is yet another example of new organizational formations that bridge historic divisions between labor and society in the United States. First established by community groups in reaction to the lack of attention shown ethnic minorities by the unions, unions in certain industries now create them. For example, in the clothing industry, the widespread practice of subcontracting has resulted in the dispersal of workers to thousands of sweatshops in New York and Los Angeles and other cities where immigrant labor is plentiful. Workers' centers are community-based institutions that provide a menu of social support to immigrant workers who come from various parts of Asia and Latin America.[40] Although the centers have been built and funded by the unions representing garment workers, they are not tied to particular organizing campaigns, but rather are intended to create a general union consciousness in the breast of immigrant communities where a low-wage workforce is recruited. Workers' centers provide various legal and social services to workers, such as provision of English-language classes, assistance in addressing wage claims, legal problems with the immigration process, and so on, as well as education about the political economic arrangements in which they are ensnared.[41] After decades in which most of the labor leadership viewed immigrants with mistrust, as largely the cause of an erosion of wages and worsened conditions for native-born workers, the AFL-CIO now takes the position, in both policy and practice, that immigrants are an important factor in the revitalization of the labor movement, should be granted amnesty if they are not legal residents of the United States, and otherwise welcomed into the "House of Labor."[42]

The melding of social activism with labor activity is, slowly but surely, contributing to the makeover of labor's public face in the United States, with the persona of the social activist emerging to compete with that of the "strongman" and the bureaucrat. While it is hard to know just how widespread or significant such social perceptions will come to be, there is no doubt but that the new organizational forms are being set into motion by a cohort of leaders who differ from their predecessors in important, but in not always very obvious ways.

The number of members serving on the AFL-CIO Executive Council has been expanded from thirty-four to fifty-two, a reform that was intended to increase the presence on the council of union leaders from minority ethnic, racial, and social backgrounds (to eight) and women (to seven), while also bringing into the national leadership circle the heads of unions whose strategic significance is substantially greater than the actual size of their organization's membership. An example is Dennis Rivera, president of District 1199, the hospital and health care workers' union (now a relatively autonomous division of SEIU). Rivera is well known as a dynamic speaker and as an unusually charismatic trade union leader with Left-leaning populist politics and a history as a political activist rather than as a functionary. Also a member of the current executive council is John Wilhelm, president of HERE, a small union of 275,000 members that is strategically positioned to make crucial inroads into the largely non-union industries of restaurants and tourism. Wilhelm, fifty-five years old and a graduate of Yale, spent three decades in the background of an often corrupt and conservative union, working to transform it into one of the more aggressive and innovative unions in the nation.

Although the median age (sixty-two years) of the current ex-

"THE MANUFACTURE OF AN ACTIVIST"

The following are reflections of Virginia Yu, an organizer for the Chinese Staff and Workers Association, a workers' center located in the Chinese community of Manhattan in New York City:

I became active during the summer of 1995. There was a struggle at Jing Fong, at the time the largest Chinese restaurant in the Northeast. A worker was fired after he started asking questions and a campaign began in February 1995. I was in school, in the first year of my master's program in social work. When I came back from school in the summer, I was informed of the campaign. The campaign had come to a standstill because of collusion between the police, Chinese newspapers, the tongs (an association of businessmen with connections to the street gangs who enforce their policies), and the Chinese Restaurant Association.

I feel I should tell you about my background. My parents came here twenty-six years ago and they have been working in the factory ever since. My father worked as a button machine operator. My mother worked as a seamstress. My grandmother worked in the factory until she retired.

When I was a young child my mother worked at home. I remember when I was five or six years old, my mom sewing and my older sister helping out. My mother would bring work home from the factory. She had to go to the factory to get the garments. She would have to bring the garments back to the factory after they were sewn. My mother still tells me today how she would drag the three of us, on the train, going up and down the staircases, with this huge cart full of sewn garments.

I myself didn't start working in the factory until I was in junior

(continued)

ecutive council is unchanged from previous periods, and there are no striking differences in social background characteristics (for example, the level and kind of their educational attainment is only slightly higher than in previous cohorts), it is at the secondary level of leadership that a shift in the social trajectory of the

(continued)

high school. It was illegal for me to be working but I had to help my father. In addition, my two sisters worked there.

I remember how I, after Chinese school, would go to the factory where my father worked. This might be on a Sunday evening. I hated going there, but I had to help out as best I could. I didn't like to do the actual machine work because at the time I was so young. Sometimes my grandmother or my sisters would work with us, if the garments had to get out the next day. When my mother finished her own work, she would come help my father. We were always there. We would not leave until nine or ten in the evening.

I remember my mom coming home late and complaining of aches and pains in her shoulders, her back, her hands. Almost every night, after we ate I would give her a massage to ease her pain. After twenty years of work she developed an occupational disease and could not work for nine months. Even today, she can only work seven or eight hours a day. The sad part is that seven or eight hours is considered part-time!

My father is still working in the factory even though my sisters and I now have jobs. I had always thought that I would go to school and make enough money so that my parents didn't need to work in the factory. But my parents are still working to make sure they earn at least the $7,000 a year necessary to maintain their health insurance.

Until I found Chinese Staff, I didn't know that I could do something, that there was an organization with which I could try to change the situation of my family. Now, I realize that the only way *really* to make change is by organizing workers of all trades in the community. When I found this opportunity, I jumped in with both feet.

SOURCE: Lynd and Lynd, *New Rank and File,* pp. 250–51.

American labor leadership may be more discernible.[43] As John Sweeney acceded to the top of the AFL-CIO, he brought with him a cohort of younger militants from his home union, SEIU. Recall that SEIU had been unusual among postwar American unions for hiring leftists as organizers, and many of the radical organizers who rose through its ranks were brought in by Sweeney to head departments within the AFL-CIO administrative apparatus, thereby creating a remarkable situation in which left-wing radicals, banished to the very fringes of the labor movement for almost half a century, were suddenly invited to take seats in the inner circle.

These new militants tend to be leaders who hold appointed rather than elected positions, meaning they are often without membership constituencies of their own and serve at the pleasure of the elected president.[44] Many entered the labor movement from various social movements that were active in the 1960s and 1970s (the antiwar movement, the civil rights movement, the women's movement, and from the community organizing movement) and therefore came with experiences in social combat that were utterly foreign to most union staff members and functionaries.[45] Charged with nothing less than reversing the fortunes of a declining labor movement, and having been handed substantial resources to accomplish the feat, this group has appeared brash and overconfident to many in the labor movement. They are also perceived as somewhat "cliquish," a perception that may have some basis in their very real friendship circles, in the smallness of left-wing activist networks in the United States, and in the fact that many had worked for a single organization, SEIU.

The air of arrogance and exclusivity that they sometimes give off is compounded by the fact that the political will for many of the dramatic changes that have occurred in the labor movement have come from the top, not the rank and file who are usually believed to be the only source of democratic change. Steve Lerner, a key strategist for SEIU's Justice for Janitors campaigns and one of the young activists brought in by Sweeney, unapologetically asserts that a key element of SEIU's success has been the institutional decision not to tolerate local leaders who did not want to organize.[46] This approach has sharpened the hostility to college-educated "outsiders" in some quarters, although no one denies that SEIU has by far the best record of recruiting new members and of advancing the difficult but crucial process of organizational change.

Moreover, many of the men and women who came into the labor movement with activist backgrounds had been educated at elite colleges and universities; this, together with their attitudinal style, would tend to make for a closer resemblance to Silicon Valley entrepreneurs than to veteran staffers of the trade union movement. At the same time, for a movement as down in the doldrums as the U.S. labor movement has been, such social and stylistic differences may prove to be a strength, to the extent that they assist in prying open the labor movement to new initiatives and relationships. This certainly seems to be the case with regard to the labor movement's openness to intellectuals, a group whose relations to the labor movement had been severed for decades.

In what has amounted to a historic initiative, at least within the U.S. context, a genuine rapprochement has been accomplished between labor and intellectuals. Since 1995 the top leadership of the AFL-CIO, as well as the heads of certain programmatic departments within the federation (notably the Departments of Organizing, Field Mobilization, Political Action, and Corporate Affairs) have made contacts and have sought to establish strong relations with groups of progressive university professors across the United States. This effort at partnership was introduced in a series of highly publicized teach-ins held in various parts of the country in 1996 and 1997, in which intellectuals (mostly academic historians and philosophers) were brought together with labor leaders to speak on panels, jointly and publicly, with John Sweeney and several of the young militants whom he appointed to his administration.[47] The intellectuals called on for this important work of collective representation were those with a profile that was high and a politics that, while critical, would not be too critical of the labor leadership itself. Previously, meaningful relations between the labor movement and intellectuals had been extremely difficult to construct because of a deep legacy of political mistrust (sustained by the cold war, the Vietnam War, strong cultural discord, and so on). But now, with the changes in the AFL-CIO, an alliance had become possible.

In the aftermath of the highly publicized teach-ins, top staff from the AFL-CIO made presentations at academic conferences and generally sought to develop a presence among academics, especially historians and sociologists. This kind of effort would have been impossible to imagine prior to the Sweeney administration. At the same time, in order to assemble the proper participants and audiences for these meetings, networks of labor-oriented academics were formed, thus demonstrating one way in which labor's new metaphysic was able to spawn new organization.[48]

The current leadership of the labor movement views the construction of such new relationships as a crucial part of the process of actually becoming a movement. Whereas the previous generation of leaders viewed intellectuals and Left activists with unrestrained contempt borne of a deep experiential and cultural divide, the new militants are at ease with intellectuals and progressive activists, with whom they share both a measure of cultural capital and a set of experiences in social struggle that conjoin them as bearers of a sacred narrative.

Let's be clear. Although the leadership of the U.S. labor movement is different from its predecessors, that doesn't mean that it is now raising a clear, frontal political challenge to the basic edifice of neoliberalism. But while its political practice at the national level has barely moved from where it has stood historically, labor practices on the ground, an important foundation of its social power, may offer a more complicated story.

CHAPTER FOUR

Practices and Possibilities of a Social Movement Unionism

In the 1990s, following years of declining membership and organizational paralysis, a few American unions quite unexpectedly began to experiment with a new, more expansive, and more combative model of unionism. This new unionism has yielded some dramatic victories. Tens of thousands of low-wage building service workers have been organized in "Justice for Janitors" campaigns, carried out in several cities by the Service Employees International Union (SEIU). SEIU also achieved a historic milestone in February 1999 when it organized 74,000 minimum-wage home health care workers in Southern California—the largest successful unionization drive in the United States since the United Automobile Workers (UAW) organized General Motors in 1937. The Hotel Employees and Restaurant Employees International Union (HERE) has similarly organized significant numbers of poorly paid hotel workers, most notably in the huge gambling casinos of Las Vegas, where in the last few years, more than 32,000 workers have become unionized. And over the past couple of years, the Union of Needletrades, Industrial and Textile Employees (UNITE) has pursued an ambitious campaign to organize America's industrial laundries, to date unionizing one-quarter of the industry.[1] Equally important, this new unionism has inspired other social movement groups to participate in labor's struggles and to undertake their own campaigns to improve the dismal state of low-wage workers in the United States. At its best, this social movement unionism has generated new and unexpected sources of social power.

These union victories and the promise they hold for stimulating broader social activism have attracted wide attention, both internationally and at home. In some places, most notably England and Australia, top union officials have championed this model, viewing it as a way to regain political and economic power for their own labor movements. Elsewhere, most conspicuously in the U.S. business press, these victories have either been ignored or dismissed as the last gasp of a dinosaur. But to judge adequately what it might portend for the future, one must appreciate that it is a response to a very specific set of constraints in American society, especially the way in which American employers have broken down labor's traditional stronghold in the goods-producing core of the U.S. economy. It is both the specific features of the employers' assault and the creativity of a new generation of labor activists in response to it that have combined to shape these victories. Only by recognizing this can one hope to understand the trajectory and potential for a new unionism in the United States.

CRISIS IN LABOR'S STRONGHOLD

Paradoxically, the new union victories of the 1990s could not have come at a more inauspicious time, for they followed more than two decades of a militant offensive by American corporate managers to destroy unions and, along with them, the private system of social provision that unions had forged in key strongholds of the manufacturing economy. As we have already seen, employers in the United States have institutional opportunities for opposing unions that are unmatched in Europe, and beginning in the 1980s, they seized on these opportunities to evade the financial costs of the private system of social provision.[2] Since American labor law provides formal mechanisms for de-unionization, something unheard of in Europe, and also allows strikebreakers to cast ballots in elections to decertify unions, employers provoked strikes in their unionized firms and then hired strikebreakers to decertify the union.[3] Because America's union election procedure makes it extraordinarily difficult for unorganized workers to unionize, allowing employers to orchestrate antiunion campaigns as part of the recognition process, employers began to move increasing amounts of investment to those plants that had no union representation (often in "right-to-work" states where labor laws are even more hostile to unions than they are nationally), and then mounted fierce union avoidance campaigns when union drives were initiated, contesting and delaying NLRB elections, firing union activists without compunction, and hiring antiunion consulting firms.[4] In taking advantage of these institutional opportunities, employers were responding to substantial incentives embedded in the American system of labor relations. Because collective bargaining is so decentralized, with no mechanisms for extending the terms of successful union negotiations to workers in other firms (as there are in Europe), employers are able to reap enormous financial gains by operating without unions; their gains are thus far unequaled in Europe. The net effect of these actions has been ruinous for labor throughout the past two decades: strike rates plummeted, union density plunged, and union election defeats multiplied.[5]

Managerial initiatives to deal with global competition added to labor's crisis in manufacturing. As corporations reorganized themselves to increase "flexibility," they began to contract out work that had previously been done within the firm and to construct strategic alliances with the contractors, creating at least three distinct difficulties for unions. First, contracting instantly de-unionized jobs because contractors were often not bound by union agreements, which governed only relationships between corporations and their direct employees. Second, contracting served to decentralize production, which meant that unions no longer dealt with a few large employers; they now had to organize and bargain with multiple employers, a much more complicated and onerous process. And third, it meant that the very conception of an "employer," enshrined in U.S. labor law, was increasingly out of step with the reality of workers' lives. NLRB procedures assumed that "employers" were distinct entities, easily defined and delineated, and that they occupied real positions of power and control over workers' lives and working conditions.[6] But in fact, these contractors were rarely so distinct, nor frequently were they the ones that held the real, immediate power over workers' existence.

Demographic shifts in the labor force and structural changes in the economy also played a role in labor's troubles. However, here too the institutional context amplified the effects. By the early 1980s, women, minorities, and immigrants were a growing portion of the labor force in America. And the jobs they held were primarily in the rapidly growing service sector, not in the shrinking manufacturing industries. Jobs in the service sector tended to be much worse—they paid less, rarely provided good health and retirement benefits, and were more often part-time or temporary positions. Although this seemed natural to most Americans, it has not been the case in many European countries where service sector wages have more closely matched manufacturing wages, and where health, pension, and other benefits are determined by legislation and tend to be applied universally to jobholders.[7] In the U.S. institutional context, however, the growth of lousy service sector jobs and the decline of good manufacturing jobs put downward pressure on wages throughout the labor force and heightened tensions between blue-collar White males who still benefited from the private system of social provision and the growing number of non-White female service workers who did not.

Thus, employers' intransigence combined with America's decentralized labor market institutions to produce an exceptionally hostile environment for unions. The areas of the economy where unions had been strong throughout the postwar period increasingly seemed to be beyond labor's organizing capacity, as employers erected what amounted to a "no-go zone" in many parts of the manufacturing economy where unions had earlier built what was, in essence, a private welfare state. Outside these sectors of the economy, conditions also appeared bleak. Most notably, in the growing service sector, both the workforce and work conditions differed dramatically, and unions had no experience and few footholds from which to launch new initiatives. The only area of hope for the labor movement was the public sector, where a combination of political and social pressures could be used to prevent public employers from running the kinds of aggressive antiunion campaigns seen in the private sector.

Outside this public sector, union leaders vacillated between surrender and denial as they confronted the new reality. One sign of surrender was the virtual cessation of organizing efforts as unions discovered that the tactics they had relied on for decades, especially National Labor Relations Board (NLRB) elections, stopped yielding victories. By 1985, only .1 percent of the private-sector workforce was organized through NLRB elections on an annual basis, a minuscule number, especially in the context of massive de-unionization.[8]

But even more ominous was the fact that most top labor leaders denied the crisis altogether. For years, as the situation grew steadily worse, those at the helm of the AFL-CIO held fast to the attitude of George Meany, who in the 1970s remarked, "Why should we worry about organizing. . . . Frankly I used to worry about the membership, about the size of membership. But quite a few years ago, I just stopped worrying about it, because to me, it doesn't make any difference."[9] Other leaders spoke of "circling the wagons" or "riding out the storm." And then there were those who simply wished the crisis away by reinterpreting their union's jurisdiction to include only the subsectors where they still had members. For example, the United Automobile Workers simply ignored new auto parts contractors, all of whom opened up nonunion enterprises, and local officials of the United Food and Commercial Workers Union began to redefine their jurisdiction so that department stores, which they had once unionized, were no longer considered within their purview. In short, most leaders were stuck in an organizational culture that was based on an economic reality and a labor-management-government relationship that no longer existed, leaving them utterly ineffective (and powerless) in responding to the crisis.[10]

The political ramifications of this surrender and denial only intensified the crisis. As union leaders sought ever more fervently to protect and service their shrinking membership base, they had less and less incentive to speak for a broader working class. And when they made the effort, it was easily discredited, as the dwindling size of unions along with their unrepresentative demography buttressed the argument that the labor movement was just a narrow, privileged interest group, a despised category in American political culture.

By the late 1980s, then, the collapse of the U.S. labor movement seemed only a matter of time. Even labor's supporters began to predict that by the turn of the millennium union density would drop below 5 percent, causing labor's political voice and its institutional presence to essentially vanish altogether.[11] American employers had successfully created a no-go zone in the very areas of the economy where labor had once achieved its greatest successes. With private industry now essentially beyond labor's organizing capacity, this pessimistic scenario seemed all but inevitable.

NEW PRACTICES, NEW POSSIBILITIES

Against this backdrop of organizational decline and paralysis, a small number of union activists, all working for unions outside the manufacturing sector, began to experiment with new approaches to organizing workers. Avoiding the core goods-producing center of the American economy, these activists focused their efforts on rebuilding the labor movement in the service and public sectors, which often entailed organizing immigrant, minority, and women workers, previously written off as unorganizable. Their actions challenged the received wisdom of business unionism in other ways as well, especially by their more critical stance toward neoliberalism and their insistence that the goal of organizing was not merely to increase the numbers of workers in unions, but to get workers to assert their own collective power directly when dealing with employers. Yet, unlike in the 1930s when militants created new organizational vehicles to change the labor movement, these activists were working from within the very union structures that had long sustained business unionism; in short they tried to build a new labor movement within the shell of the old. The hallmarks of their approach have been flexibility and the way in which they have attempted to circumvent bureaucratic union structures and state-sponsored channels for managing labor conflict.

More specifically, the new unionism can be characterized by the half-dozen ways in which its practices tend to contrast with those of business unionism: first, rather than trying to organize the unorganized with campaigns directed from the top that "sell" unions as a kind of representational service that will benefit those who purchase it, social movement unionists have focused instead on attempting to build unions as organizational vehicles of social solidarity, so that workers will have the means for *collectively* solving the problems they face at work and in society. Organizing within this framework means engaging workers face to face, promoting rank-and-file leadership, teaching workers how to create workplace committees that involve workers themselves in the tasks of organizing, and emphasizing direct action as an important source of collective power. The contrast with the servicing model of unionism is sharp and deliberate: as one prominent AFL-CIO activist put it, "Instead of lowering the definition of what it means to be a union member—cheap benefits, another credit card—we are saying that what we have is so valuable that it commands greater commitment."[12]

Second, social movement unionists rely heavily on corporate campaigns to deal with the huge power disparity in the United States between employers and employees. The corporate campaign is a tactic originally conceived by the New Left as part of its effort to end the Vietnam War; in essence, it attempts to turn key parts of a corporation's social network against it.[13] Based on extensive research, especially finding out who a company's lenders, clients, shareholders, and subsidiaries are, potential pressure points are identified and then used in an escalating campaign to overcome employer opposition. For instance, a union's corporate campaign might begin by identifying church groups that have dealings with a company that may be fighting a unionization drive by its workers; the union would then develop a public campaign to expose the hypocrisy between the church's principals and the company's in an effort to get the church group to pressure the company to cease its opposition to unionism. Then, to escalate this pressure, the union might conduct research on the company's subsidiaries, publicizing any damaging information it might uncover, such as a problematic health and safety record, or irregular pricing policies. All information that potentially jeopardizes the employers' relations with customers, investors, politicians, or regulators is considered fair and reasonable in a corporate campaign. At root, it is a tactic that assumes a fundamental antagonism between corporations and unions; for this very reason, it was once shunned by labor leaders in the United States, but it fits well with the larger critique of U.S. capitalism with which social movement unionism is now willing to be identified.

Third, social movement unionism is able and willing to look beyond the traditional and routinized form of labor recognition relied on for so long by U.S. unions, the formal NLRB election. Using either political pressure or a corporate campaign, or both, social movement unionism is prepared to push for recognition from employers based solely on getting 50 percent plus one of the workers to sign a card saying that they want union recognition. This is called "card-check recognition" and may not seem particularly radical, especially since it is the state-sanctioned procedure in countries like Canada and England, but such is the environment in the United States that when workers circumvent the bureaucratic channels to demand direct union recognition from their employer, it constitutes a genuine act of defiance. As part of this more militant strategy, unions often ask community or religious leaders to certify the card count. In using this tactic, social movement unions not only avoid a process that is stacked against them, but also gain a degree of leverage because employers are unnerved by a procedure that they are unable to manipulate as effectively as the NLRB system.

Fourth, social movement unionism has a strong orientation toward social justice, rhetorically connecting labor movement revival to a broader movement for expanded democracy and social citizenship in the United States and to anticorporate struggles internationally. Traditional union concerns like wages and benefits are still acknowledged and made the object of social struggle, but these are now expressly linked to broader discourses of social dignity and universal civil rights. This is an important alternative to the cold pragmatism of what was once termed "bread and butter unionism."

Fifth, its style is creative; strategic innovation and experimentation of all kinds are highly valued rather than squelched. Activists believe that in view of the hostile legal context, there can be no formula, no predictability, and that employers must be kept off guard, not knowing what to expect. Thus organizers must not become wedded to any one set of tactics, but rather must be willing to quickly devise new techniques as employers learn to neutralize old ones. Activists also argue that using multiple tactics increases the possibility of generating a crisis, which can then serve as leverage to achieve workers' demands. This too puts a premium on experimentation and innovation.

Finally, social movement unionism is self-expanding, carrying with it a strong sense that successes *and* defeats occur in the context of a long-term process. Successes are interpreted to demonstrate that social movement unionism *can* succeed despite the hostile economic and legal climate. Failures are interpreted as spurs to greater ingenuity. So, for instance, when an organizing campaign to unionize janitors met with defeat when it tried to organize subcontractors, who under U.S. law are the employers of record, activists decided that in the next campaign they would redefine "employer" as the corporate entities that ultimately held real power over workers' lives and find ways to target them. For social movement unionists, every campaign, triumph or failure, is seen as building to the next one. In other words, unionism is practiced as a *movement*.

The social dynamic of this new unionism represents a sharp

departure from the narrow, insular tendency of business unionism. Rather than centering conflict only at the point of production or service provision, the arena of conflict is expanded to en-
compass the community and larger society. Churches and
progressive groups are called on to live up to their principals by
pressuring companies with which they do business; priests and
community leaders are prevailed upon to certify card-check elections; and community members are persuaded to side with workers in struggles that disrupt everyday life, rather than with authorities trying to end the disruption. Indeed, social movement
unionism encourages a new culture of solidarity, as its approach
to organizing requires that larger and larger segments of the
community be brought into the effort to win basic rights for
workers, particularly those most marginalized and vulnerable in
the new economy. Moreover, the vision of labor evoked by social
movement unionism is entirely different than the one conjured
up by business unionism: unions are seen as dealing with questions of social justice that extend well beyond the unionized
workforce, rather than advocating only for a narrow interest
group. Indeed, one reason for the success of social movement
unionism in the overwhelmingly hostile environment of U.S.
labor relations is that it allows organizers to evoke a new vision of
unionism that contrasts dramatically with old-style business
unionism of workers' experience and cultural memory.[14] It also
draws American unionism much closer to European practices of
unionism and therefore points to, among other things, the rather
slender reed upon which the trope of American labor exceptionalism has been built.

Once John Sweeney became president of the AFL-CIO in
1995 the new leadership undertook several initiatives intended to

prod the other member unions to devote substantial resources toward organizing new members, under the banner, "Changing to Organize, Organizing to Change." Embedded in these initiatives were many of the practices of social movement unionism. For example, Sweeney created an Organizing Department, designed to provide strategic assistance to member unions and to coordinate large-scale, multiunion organizing projects in various parts of the country, several of which have emerged as experimental models for both cross-union and union-community organization and solidarity. To supply the staff demanded by this effort, funding was increased for the Organizing Institute, whose mission is to systematically train a new generation of labor organizers, drawn from both student and worker ranks. Recruiting students into the labor movement has required establishing ongoing links to university campuses, ethnic communities, and religious organizations, something that Sweeney and other leaders of the AFL-CIO have actively facilitated, in sharp contrast to the insularity and mistrust that often characterized relationships between these groups and AFL-CIO leaders in the past. They began an annual "Union Summer" program, which brings hundreds of students and workers into organizing campaigns for several weeks each summer. The program's very name symbolically links the labor movement with the historic civil rights movement, for it evokes the mantle of "Freedom Summer," one of the most famous events of the 1960s, when northern college students went to the South to participate in the fight for Black equality. In making this link, the program seeks to represent unions to young people as being "hip" in stylistic terms and as a worthy moral cause with which to be associated.[15] The more recent 2003

Immigrant Workers Freedom Ride, also supported by the AFL-CIO, is another deliberate echo of the 1960s.

The Sweeney administration also challenged national unions to devote 30 percent of their budgets to organizing, because they understood that if unions committed so much to organizing, they would be forced to fundamentally alter the way that unionism would be practiced. In 1995, most unions were spending only 2 or 3 percent of their budgets on new organizing. The only way to meet the 30 percent goal would be for union staff to do less of the servicing and grievance handling, relying more on members' collective action, thus spurring a radical change in the culture of local unions.[16]

However, even with the changed programs of the AFL-CIO and the impressive growth achieved by SEIU (now the largest national union in the United States), the task of building social movement unions remains formidable. Foremost, enormous resources are lined up against it on the employers' side, especially in manufacturing, where businesses are determined not to accept union organization, and where employers wield a credible threat to move overseas if workers unionize. (Recall that in the United States employers are legally free to move anywhere, on short notice, without paying severance costs, and they do so frequently.) But resistance is also strong within both local and national unions, where many leaders and members remain bound to a business union model and the "servicing" mentality that it creates. They can be expected to resist the AFL-CIO's initiatives until social movement unions prove that they are able to really hold back the tide of de-unionization. Indeed, today only six of the sixty-five national unions affiliated with the AFL-CIO are vigorously pursuing the new organizing agenda. These six represent about one-third of the AFL-CIO's total membership, but even within these unions, there are many locals that resist adopting the new union practices.[17] Moreover, the power of the AFL-CIO to compel its affiliates to do anything is quite limited; unlike labor federations in European countries, it is a decentralized, voluntary federation of affiliated unions with no actual members of its own. Although this decentralization was important for allowing the revitalization process to begin (without it unions like SEIU would never have been able to organize as effectively as they did, on their own, during the 1980s and early 1990s), it is a knife that cuts both ways, for now that the AFL-CIO leadership is in support of a comprehensive revitalization, is has few means by which to force other affiliated organizations to adopt the practices that would accomplish it.

The road to a social movement unionism and a revitalized American labor movement is indeed proving to be very difficult, and success is by no means assured. However, the promise of social movement unionism in the United States is substantial, as can be seen in the way that it has transformed power and politics in the unlikeliest of settings: among low-paid janitorial and hotel workers in the two American cities that are most closely identified as symbols of capitalist excess: Los Angeles and Las Vegas.

A "CASE OF THE POSSIBLE" IN LOS ANGELES

If there is one set of organizing campaigns that best demonstrates the promise of social movement unionism, it is the Justice for Janitors (J for J) campaign, initiated in the mid-1980s when John Sweeney was president of SEIU.[18] The story of the campaign serves as allegory, for nearly all the actors in the current American workscape are represented within it: rapacious, capitalist investors; precarious, poorly paid, contract workers; large numbers of economically and legally vulnerable immigrant workers; radical union reformers; entrenched, "old-guard" union oligarchies; a large and growing body of sympathetic community activists; and at the heart of it all, the increasing visibility of open class conflict between the winners and losers in the contemporary American economy.

SEIU started in 1920 as a union of janitors who cleaned commercial buildings. Beginning in the 1960s, it expanded into health care and the public sector, both growing areas of employment, where the union began to organize clerical and professional workers in addition to janitors. This expansion into new sectors enabled SEIU to grow in an era when other U.S. unions were losing members and cushioned the large membership losses that hit when corporate restructuring began to transform the janitorial industry. Historically, janitors had been direct employees of building owners or their managers, and the union had typically bargained with citywide associations of owners, most of whom were homegrown capitalists. Under these conditions, the union had built powerful locals in many commercial centers. But this arrangement broke down in the 1980s, as commercial development first boomed and then went bust, sending rental rates spiraling downward and replacing local owners with national and international investors.[19] Building managers started contracting out the cleaning of their buildings, often to nonunion contractors, and when they did, wages and working conditions plummeted. Further undermining janitors' pay and working conditions was the international character of the recession of the

1980s, which produced a large influx of immigrant workers who had few employment choices other than working for nonunion cleaning contractors. Nowhere were these factors as acute as in Los Angeles.

Overcoming the many obstacles to unionization in this context required new approaches, something that was unlikely to emerge among the old-guard leaders of SEIU janitor locals, most of whom had held office for years and were very resistant to change. Traditionally, SEIU local unions enjoyed a great deal of autonomy, and staff were able to run their local unions without much interference from the national office, a situation that, had it continued, would have eventually resulted in the complete de-unionization of business services. However, when John Sweeney became president of SEIU, he began to move toward centralizing the union, succeeding largely because SEIU's expansion into the public sector gave it a growing treasury and brought a more liberal membership into the union, both of which supported his efforts. In addition to increasing the size of the national staff, Sweeney proved willing to use "trusteeship"—the power to temporarily take over the affairs of locals when the local leadership was corrupt or incompetent—to advance a much more aggressive organizing agenda. The Justice for Janitors campaign was the brainchild of this new national staff, many of whom came to SEIU as seasoned veterans of progressive social movements, and they often used mechanisms like trusteeships to circumvent oligarchic local leaders who obstructed organizing initiatives.[20]

The first place the national SEIU staff tried out the J for J campaign was in Denver, Colorado, where it launched an organizing effort that was focused on building a social movement, instead of merely getting janitors to sign union cards requesting an

NLRB election. A two-pronged strategy was used: one focused on overcoming labor's long dependence on a union contract to represent workers; the other aimed at mobilizing community and public support. To organize the janitors without the NLRB and without a contract, the J for J staff used guerrilla-style legal maneuvers, charging contractors with violations of health and safety regulations and pressuring state agencies to live up to their legal obligations to protect workers. The goal was to demonstrate to workers that a union could bring advantages even without attaining formal legal status. To build community support, the J for J activists initiated a media-savvy exposure of employers' abuses in one Denver building, highlighting the ways in which contractors' violated janitors' civil and human rights. But the SEIU staff soon discovered that a "movement" approach by itself was not enough to mobilize the workers. Janitors simply were not willing to risk their livelihoods when the target was a single building, for they knew that even if the union succeeded, the contractor for that building could then simply be underbid by someone else. Only when the SEIU staff came up with a strategy to simultaneously target a larger group of downtown buildings did the janitors give their full support to the campaign. In the end, the campaign yielded only modest gains, but in the context of general union decline, the J for J strategists were able to frame even modest gains as a big success.[21]

Then, in a bold move in 1988, the SEIU organizing staff took the J for J campaign to Los Angeles, California. Los Angeles was a much larger and more difficult arena, with many thousands more janitors and hundreds more contractors than Denver, and it also was a city with a long antiunion history, a boomtown devoted to low wages and "industrial freedom," code words in the

United States for "no labor unions."[22] As one SEIU staffer put it, "Going from Denver to monstrous LA was . . . really huge," and the staff wondered if they were really ready for it.[23] However, SEIU's expansion into the public sector, especially in California, gave it a fair amount of political leverage in the city, and that made the prospect of tackling the nonunion bastion somewhat less daunting than it otherwise would have been. In Los Angeles, the J for J staff encountered a workforce that was almost entirely made up of immigrants, many of them without official documents and illegally residing in the country. Earlier in the decade, a huge influx of destitute Latinos had flooded into Los Angeles, and building managers had taken advantage of their vulnerability, terminating agreements with the existing unionized workforce (chiefly African Americans) and signing new contracts with subcontractors who employed immigrants for less than half of what their unionized predecessors had been paid. According to the conventional wisdom of the time, these immigrants were "unorganizable."[24] The widely held assumption was that illegal, undocumented immigrants lacked any real potential as union recruits. They were thought to view their situation in relation to their home countries, where conditions were even worse, and they were vulnerable to deportation and thus fearful of any confrontation with authority. Moreover, while almost all the undocumented immigrants in Los Angeles were Latino, they came from different nations, such as Mexico, El Salvador, and Guatemala, and felt little affinity for each other.[25]

Los Angeles also presented difficulties because local labor leaders were habituated to business unionism. The SEIU local with jurisdiction over the janitors (Local 399) had given up trying to organize them; instead, the leadership spent its time servicing existing union members, most of whom were employed in the health care industry. The leadership was suspicious of the J for J effort, in part because they recognized that a sudden infusion of new, immigrant members might jeopardize their political position in the local. Thus the national union administration essentially imposed the J for J campaign on the local, creating tension throughout the organizing drive.[26]

Drawing on their experience in Denver, the first thing the J for J staffers did was design a corporate campaign against Los Angeles's janitorial industry. A full-time, university-trained researcher went to work gathering information—later supplemented by researchers in the national office—about the ownership and the management structure of the commercial cleaning business in Los Angeles. The research produced a visual and statistical tableau of the industry, something that had previously been the exclusive province of the industry itself. It provided information, for example, about the incredibly large differences in wage rates across different regions, cities, and suburbs, and showed that many companies were "double-breasted," that is, they were operating both unionized and nonunionized units of workers, with substantial differences between them. This served as a powerful organizing tool in dramatically demonstrating the benefits that union membership could bring.[27]

The research also identified the people who held real power in the industry. Since the J for J staff planned from the outset to circumvent the official NLRB channel to union representation, they were not constrained by its narrow legalistic definition of the "employer" and were instead free to design a corporate campaign targeting the institutional actors who really held power over workers' lives. The research revealed that the real power holders were not the small, fly-by-night subcontractors. Instead, there were two key players in the industry: the actual owners of the properties being cleaned and the large building service corporations (based in locales as far away as Denmark and Belize and merging so quickly that it was often hard to keep up-to-date on actual ownership) who were usually the ultimate cosigners of union contracts. Building owners were not only at the top of this economic food chain, as the final customer of the services that the janitors provided, but they were also the most vulnerable to public opinion and social disruption because their profits depended on maintaining the prestigious reputation of their properties and keeping the vacancy rate low. Furthermore—and this illustrated the genius of the J for J researchers—the owners of buildings were very likely to concede defeat before the building service contractors themselves, simply because an agreement with the union costs them *less* proportionately. That is, janitors' wages cost the owner/manager only about 5 cents out of each dollar collected from rent. Union wages may raise these costs to the owner by a penny or two—perhaps not even enough to be passed on in the form of higher rents to the tenants—but wages and other benefits represent a much larger portion of the service contractor's operating funds, thus making him much less likely to give in to union demands. Targeting building owners would therefore convert what had been a great liability for labor—the ultraflexible outsourcing system and the sheer size of capital's operations—into a strategic advantage, something analogous to vulnerable pressure points on an opponent's body. Moreover, the owners' interests were so ambiguously linked to those of the out-sourced contractors that they were likely to more easily give in to union demands. The entire system was so centralized and vertically integrated that victory at the top would pour instantly, inexorably down through the system to the worker, like water off a roof. Even the thirty-day notice-bidding system could be subverted. Once the J for J campaign had assured the security of the workers in the building by pressuring building owners into agreeing to retain the building's present cleaners, activists could then push relentlessly to get the building's owner to hand the contractor a thirty-day ultimatum, basically amounting to "go union or you're fired."

The strategy seems so elegantly simple in retrospect, but as one of the key J for J strategists put it, simplicity is often incredibly complicated.[28] Clever targeting, while essential, was not itself enough to bring victory. Ultimately, to achieve success, the janitors themselves had to be mobilized. Here, too, research played a role, for it showed workers how and why they could potentially win. Once the janitors understood the big picture—and the J for J staff spent a lot of time educating them—they too saw that pressuring the building owners and big contractors was a key to victory. Moreover, research helped motivate action because it made the janitors angry to see how little it would actually cost building owners to pay them better wages: as one of the J for J staff noted, workers tend to "get pissed off when they learn that it costs one cent to give them a raise."[29]

Besides research, the J for J staff expanded on the guerrilla-style legal maneuvers they had used in Denver. They aggressively filed "unfair labor practice" complaints every time a contractor threatened a union supporter, and they generally tried to economically pressure the cleaning contractors by upping the fees they had to pay their lawyers. In addition, the J for J activists relied heavily on disruptive, nonviolent direct action to build support in Los Angeles. For example, they designed a series of demonstrations to bring the city's poorest workers into direct contact with the affluent world of the corporate tycoons who owned and rented the office buildings. One protest, for example, took place at a golf course, where the workers chanted and carried signs that publicized the poverty wages they received for cleaning up after rich CEOs and their well-paid lawyers. In another action, workers came out to perform street theater in front of an expensive Los Angeles restaurant while the owner of a contracting firm dined inside. Such actions represented public "shaming rituals" that fostered community support by underscoring the injustice of the poverty wages of the janitors in relation to the ostentatious wealth of the building inhabitants.[30]

At first, the demonstrations were deliberately calculated to maximize media coverage while minimizing risks to workers; only later did organizers ask workers to engage in actions that might expose them to the possibility of arrest or losing their jobs. The point was to build up the collective confidence of the janitors to the point where they had a good understanding of the real gains to be made by joining a union and by making trouble, and the inevitable trade off in commitment and risk that both decisions involved. Then, as public pressure on the owners and contractors built, along with worker confidence, the J for J activists escalated the conflict by encouraging workers to engage in riskier acts of civil disobedience, like sitting down in the lobbies of buildings and refusing to budge, or barging into sensitive business meetings, chanting loudly, and tossing bags of trash.

The J for J campaign also relied on political pressure. In the 1980s a commercial building boom was underway in Los Angles but before construction could begin, developers needed approval from the city's Community Redevelopment Authority. The J for J staff cultivated political allies with leverage in that approval process.[31]

These tactics yielded victories at several downtown buildings but left the centers of real power—and especially the posh Central City office complex—untouched. So in 1989, the J for J campaign targeted a multinational cleaning company that employed a large proportion of janitors in Central City, the Danish-based International Service System (ISS). For a year, the janitors pursued the same tactics against ISS that had produced their earlier successes, but these were inadequate in the battle with ISS. The janitors then voted to stage a strike, which escalated the conflict dramatically. Marches took place every day, with strikers parading along the highway and tying up traffic. The strikers were often joined by community supporters, who formed their own organization—Solidarity with Justice for Janitors—revealing the power of the J for J campaign to inspire other social actors.[32] Tensions quickly mounted, and the police began to preemptively arrest people taking part in peaceful demonstrations, citing their "suspicion" that people planned to block doors and traffic. (In other words, the police didn't wait for people to actually block doorways or traffic; they simply arrested them on the suspicion that they might.) The resulting arrests brought a great deal of publicity and more support for the janitors.[33]

A crucial turning point occurred three weeks into the strike when the police attacked demonstrators at a peaceful march. In front of TV cameras, the police wounded several people, including children and pregnant women. Widespread condemnation of the police followed, and both the mayor of Los Angeles and unions representing janitors in other cities began to pressure ISS to settle the conflict. Most significantly, the struggle finally spurred Gus Bevona, the old-guard president of the janitor's SEIU local in New York City, where ISS buildings were unionized, to act. In the past, he had been unwilling to exert any pressure on ISS on behalf of the janitors in Los Angeles, but now, in the face of the boldness of the janitors in Los Angeles, his lack of solidarity was becoming an embarrassment, especially because he was facing a significant dissident challenge in his own local.[34] Under pressure, Bevona called the president of ISS to threaten chaos in their New York buildings if a settlement was not reached in Los Angeles. A contract with janitors in Los Angeles was signed that day, granting pay increases, health insurance, vacations, and sick pay, along with union recognition. Within a remarkably short time, 90 percent of the janitors who cleaned Los Angeles's major high rises were unionized.[35]

It was a clear-cut victory for the workers, and it immediately catapulted Los Angeles's janitors to the front lines of the effort to redefine the meaning of unionism in the United States. The campaign illustrated the power of confrontation and strategic targeting to clear a path out of the wreckage of union decline, while simultaneously revealing the power of social movement unionism to spark levels of public support for labor not seen since the heyday of the CIO. Moreover, the campaign uncovered unexpected levels of solidarity and daring on the part of Los Angeles's immigrant janitors. Far from being the docile wage slaves that many union officials predicted and that employers smugly expected, immigrant janitors proved to be quite militant, capable of quickly marshaling support not only among their fellow janitors but also among family, friends, and neighbors. Everyone, from employer-side lawyers to old-guard officials to the J for J staff, was astonished at these workers' willingness to overtake the paid J for J staff members in their intensity and commitment.

Such militancy and solidarity dramatically challenged the belief that immigrants were unorganizable. It soon became clear that the social realities of immigrant lives could actually facilitate collective action under the right kind of circumstances, like those created by the J for J campaign. Immigrant workers relied heavily on ethnic networks for social support and for the necessities of everyday life like jobs and housing. Whereas these networks had been used in the past by contractors to recruit compliant immigrant janitors, the J for J campaign demonstrated that these same social connections could also serve as resources for building solidarity.[36] The AFL-CIO eventually reversed its long-held anti-immigrant stance as a direct outgrowth of the janitors' victory in Los Angeles.

The Justice for Janitors campaign also revealed the scale of mobilization required to overcome the overwhelming institutional advantages enjoyed by employers in the United States. The stunning victory of the janitors in 1990 was not by itself enough to turn Los Angeles into a union bastion, but it was a powerful fulcrum that pushed the city farther in that direction than anyone had thought possible. For one thing, it suddenly seemed possible that the city's vast population of foreign-born, low-wage workers could become unionized. Inspired by the janitors' success, several campaigns to organize immigrant workers have since been launched, including ones to organize wheel makers, garment workers, construction workers, truck drivers, and home health care workers. Many of these campaigns have been turned back, but one, the effort to unionize 74,000 home health care workers (workers sent to visit patients in their homes) resulted in the labor movements' largest victory since the 1930s.[37]

Another effect of the janitors' 1990 victory was that it unleashed a dynamic that eventually breathed new life into the Los Angeles Federation of Labor (known as LA FED), the local central labor council. In the past, the LA FED was like other central labor councils in postwar America: dominated by conservative building-trades unions and doing little to cultivate solidarity across trade and ethnic lines, or to build real political power for the labor movement. But after the J for J success, it became one of the most important forces in Southern California politics. In 1996, the janitors were key supporters of the first Latino ever to be elected to head the LA FED, Miguel Contreras. Working in concert, the janitors and the LA FED coordinated a widespread Latino political mobilization in Los Angeles and, in the process, have radically transformed the political balance of forces.[38] These organizing and political successes demonstrate that social movement unionism is—at least sometimes—capable of revealing new and unexpected sources of social power.

At the same time, however, events after the victory also exposed some of the sources of resistance to revitalization in U.S. unions, even in the more progressive unions like SEIU. Indeed, internal resistance within SEIU Local 399 that originally had responsibility for organizing the janitors came close to halting the development of a social movement unionism in Los Angeles. The leaders of Local 399 found it impossible to share power and fought all efforts to transform the local into an organization that might accommodate the kind of meaningful rank-and-file mobilization that janitors had used to achieve their victory over employers. In the years following the entry of the Latino janitors into 399, the local was plagued by internal factionalism. Eventually, the janitors had to use the kinds of tactics they had earlier used against the employers to try to create internal change in Local 399: they declared a hunger strike and set up camp in the union parking lot, resolving to remain there until they won real political power in the local. But even this was not enough to change Local 399; instead, it took intervention from the national office to reach a resolution. Sweeney, in one of his last acts before leaving the presidency of SEIU to become the president of the AFL-CIO, placed the local into trusteeship, and this trusteeship eventually cleared the way for the Los Angeles janitors to leave Local 399 and join other janitors in a statewide union local established just for janitors. Once this happened, the janitors were finally able to build a union that meaningfully involved workers in making decisions and running the union, revealing the extent to which the growth of social movement unionism depends on internal union reform.[39]

In April 2000 the Los Angeles janitors launched a second strike that revealed the expansive power social movement unionism can wield to generate new practices of solidarity and to draw new social actors into labor conflicts. To support the janitors, the LA FED initiated a bargaining-support campaign that turned the city's labor movement into a mutual-aid society for all the local unions whose contracts were set to expire in 2000.[40] It established a food bank and pledged to provide a weekly shopping bag for every worker on strike. And it encouraged individual unions to come to the active assistance of the janitors. Several unions supported the janitors, including a few like the Teamsters and the Operating Engineers that had never before shown solidarity with unskilled workers.[41]

Moreover, new groups were now invested in the janitors' struggle. Since 1990, the janitors had become the most politically active union in town and had been instrumental in the election of several politicians to office. Thus in the strike, janitors had support from most elected officials, including members of the state legislature, the entire city council, and even the Republican mayor. The support was substantial: council members were arrested for civil disobedience; state legislative members sat in on bargaining sessions; and national politicians addressed rallies, often wearing red J for J t-shirts. A wide array of religious and community leaders also lent their support, with many of them also being arrested for civil disobedience in support of the strike. After seventeen days, the janitors won a significant settlement from the largest building service contractors in the county, demonstrating again that the social movement unionism of the janitors could muster enough power to triumph over the dominant employer in the service sector. In the process a new public persona was created for the Los Angeles labor movement.[42]

The movement that the J for J campaign started continues to grow in Los Angles. Shortly after the 2000 strike, janitors and other immigrant workers walked picket lines in support of the city's bus drivers, who are predominately African American. Their support was especially notable because Los Angeles's changing economy has often pitted Black and immigrant workers against each other. Black workers have lost jobs (many of them well-paying manufacturing jobs), while immigrant workers have found jobs (albeit low-paying service sector jobs). These economic shifts have often led to tension, expressed on a day-to-day level on the city buses, where typically African Americans are the drivers and immigrant workers are the riders. Thus it was remarkable that when the bus drivers struck over wage cuts and efforts to privatize the bus system, the two groups made common cause, brokered in part by the County Labor Federation. Part of the reason it could happen is that over the last decade in Los Angeles, new groups have been created (a bilingual Bus Riders Union, in this case) and new social spaces opened up (like on the bus drivers' picket lines and in public meetings to pressure the Los Angeles city council to pass proworker ordinances) where different groups of workers and various types of community activists have been able to come together, have debated issues, and have worked cooperatively on these struggles. In the process they have begun to enact a new type of labor movement.[43]

In Los Angeles, then, we have witnessed the transformative promise of social movement unionism and the potential that it embodies for turning a notoriously antiunion city into a national model for service worker unionism. In the late 1980s when the J for J campaign began in Los Angeles, the terrain looked unpromising, but by 2000, Los Angeles had become an object lesson in how a union can contribute to changing the living standards—and lives—of poor workers in the United States. Los Angeles also points to ways in which the new style of unionism is able to bring new collective actors into the struggles, as occurred with the political mobilization of new immigrant voters and the newfound practices of solidarity that were demonstrated in the latest janitors' and bus drivers' strikes.

The recent history of labor in Los Angeles also reveals some of the difficulties social movement unionism has encountered. Los Angeles is currently the largest center for manufacturing employment in the United States, and yet little progress has been made in organizing the largely immigrant manufacturing workforce. This suggests that even the most progressive unions and central labor councils are thus far unable to amass sufficient power or deploy the kinds of effective strategies that might be capable of penetrating the "no-go zone" that the manufacturing sector has become for American unions. Moreover, the history of SEIU Local 399 highlights some of the ways that the organizational legacies of business unionism can serve to derail social movement unionism. At the same time, however, the experience of the city of Las Vegas, just across the Mojave Desert from Los Angeles, seemingly demonstrates the very opposite: that social movement practices are capable of cleansing some of the most corrupt and reactionary forms of unionism.

ORGANIZING LAS VEGAS

The example of Las Vegas offers another "case of the possible," for here too social movement unionism has fundamentally altered the social and political terrain in a place where such a transformation would have seemed inconceivable even a short while ago. For years Las Vegas was one of the few places where unionism actually resembled the corrupt "Mafia" caricature that U.S. employers have habitually invoked to defeat unionization drives. The roots of the corruption go back to James Hoffa Sr., who, as president of the Teamsters Union in the 1950s and 1960s, used his union's pension funds to help finance the development of Las Vegas in a period when banks were unwilling to invest in something as unsavory as gambling. Part of the arrangement that Hoffa made was that Las Vegas teamsters and hotel workers would receive good contracts and better-than-average pay, while the gambling bosses got a reliable workforce, a tractable union, and ready access to capital.[44]

This situation began to change in the mid-1970s when corporate financiers began to invest heavily in Las Vegas, taking over investments originally developed by Mafia interests. The new moneymen were unwilling, however, to take over the corrupt relationship with the hotel workers' union (HERE Local 226), and they adopted an increasingly antiunion stance. The symbiotic relationship between the union leaders and the Mafia also began to disintegrate, not so much over labor issues as over financial ones. According to a U.S. Senate investigation of racketeering, Mafia gangsters attempted to steal money from the union's health care fund and the local union leader, Al Bramlett, who had previously maintained a close relationship to the gangsters, resisted. In 1977 he was kidnapped and shot to death just outside Las Vegas.[45]

The union that Bramlett left behind, with its legacy of member passivity and behind-the-scenes deals, was ill prepared to challenge the antiunion practices of the giant corporations, which were beginning to transform Las Vegas from a haven of illicit pursuits ("Sin City") into a mass-market family-vacation spot, and sought to support this effort by cutting labor costs. Emboldened by the antiunion atmosphere of the early 1980s, the era of Ronald Reagan, and goaded by the competitive threat of legalized gambling in other parts of the United States, casino corporate owners organized themselves into the Nevada Resort Association and set out to eliminate the union from the casinos, hotels, and restaurants of Las Vegas. They came very close to accomplishing their goal in 1984, when they provoked a strike, imported strikebreakers to keep the casinos operating, persuaded a local judge to furnish an injunction to forbid picketing, and then summoned the police to arrest the nine hundred workers who defied the injunction.[46]

Even without the liability of past corruption, many local unions in the 1980s collapsed when confronted with comparable levels of intransigence and repression. Local 226 would probably have met a similar fate had it not been for the actions of HERE's national director of organizing, Vincent Sirabella, and his team of professional organizers. HERE, like SEIU, began as an AFL craft union of relatively unskilled workers. It is a highly decentralized organization with a strong tradition of local autonomy, a structure that tends to accommodate both corruption and innovation. Unlike SEIU, however, HERE was not led by a reformer like Sweeney, nor was it a growing union. Thus the organizational space for innovation was much smaller, as were the resources. But within this space, Sirabella and a few others, such as John Wilhelm, who today leads the union, had by 1984 begun to experiment with new ways of organizing workers and alternative models of unionism. Most importantly, in the early 1980s, Wilhelm initiated a highly inventive and successful campaign to organize female clerical workers at Yale University. That campaign, which lasted for four years and involved a group of workers that the union had never before tried to organize, was especially creative in promoting rank-and-file leadership in the actual running of the campaign.[47] Reporters at the time noted the "immense solidarity" of the workers, and the techniques developed in the Yale campaign for creating effective committees of "rank-and-file" workers have continued to provide a model for many HERE activists today.[48]

In response to the desperate situation of Local 226, a team of organizers was dispatched to Las Vegas, including some who had worked on the Yale campaign. They, along with several rank-and-file workers who had been radicalized by their recent experiences of mass arrest and facing down imported strikebreakers, rallied the seventeen thousand workers who were on strike to sustain the fight. They eventually won a settlement with almost all the hotels and casinos involved in the conflict. This experience—of winning gains through direct confrontation with authorities—would prove effective again and again in subsequent years to rally workers in what would turn out to be a series of grueling confrontations. But while the concessions won by the union in 1984 were impressive from the viewpoint of the abysmal state of the labor movement in 1984 (and were represented as such), the local also suffered serious wounds when six large casinos managed to keep their strikebreakers and decertify the union. The HERE team of organizers realized that they would have to rebuild the union from the ground up, much as Wilhelm had successfully done at Yale University, and they made common cause with the rank-and-file strike activists. Their highest priorities were to convince the older members that, in spite of the bruising experience of the 1984 strike, the chief source of union power is direct action to extend unionism more broadly by organizing new members, rather than servicing existing union locals, and that this would be even more important than higher wages. When contract time came around again in 1989, Local 226 mounted huge, militant demonstrations so that most of the large casinos did not dare attempt union-busting actions. Moreover, Local 226 bargained for—and won in some of the largest megaresorts—contract language establishing a card-check system for future organizing drives, an unprecedented concession that would prove absolutely key for the union's future success. In American labor parlance, this is now known as "bargaining to organize," and it has become one important tactic of social movement unionists.[49] Without it, many of the hard-won victories that have turned Las Vegas into America's quintessential union town would never have been achieved.

A few casinos, however, were determined not to follow the path of those who settled with the union in 1989, and throughout most of the 1990s, Local 226 found itself locked in deadly combat with one or another of these casinos. In 1990, the union won a ten-month strike against one of them, with the help of the city's Black community, but a second strike against another, the Frontier, dragged on for more than six years and became the longest strike in postwar U.S. history. The strike involved repeated moments of high drama and solidarity: mass demonstrations of twenty thousand people, which shut down the heart of the gambling district; a 300-mile march by strikers across the Mojave Desert to publicize the strikers plight; and Local 226 members voting overwhelmingly to raise their dues by 40 percent so that the local could pay strike benefits to strikers, while continuing to devote funds to organizing new members. Throughout the entire six-year period, not a single worker ever crossed the picket line. The strike was finally won in 1998, after the AFL-CIO used its political leverage to threaten the gambling license of Frontier's owners.[50]

During the Frontier strike, Local 226 had continued to initiate campaigns to organize new members, something few other unions were doing, even when they were not also simultaneously carrying out a bitter and high-profile strike. And these campaigns, too, sometimes led to protracted battles, most notably with MGM, which in 1993 opened up what was at the time the largest casino ever built, a massive 5,005-room resort-casino combination. The new casino announced its intention to be nonunion and refused to recognize the union based on the card-check system. Overcoming MGM's opposition took years of mass demonstrations and sit-ins, made all the more confrontational by the fact that MGM claimed the sidewalk in front of the casino as private property; therefore, workers were arrested when they demonstrated in front of the club. It also took corporate research. HERE researchers are particularly well known in both labor and corporate circles for their skill at using Wall Street skills to further labor's cause, and in the case of MGM, researchers did things like combing the world of high finance to find material to pressure the company.[51] One discovery was that MGM's projected profits were grossly overestimated. The union began to circulate a report about the overestimates to spur investors to pressure MGM into ending its antiunion actions. Both the demonstrations and the research contributed to the union victory, which was announced right after the Frontier agreement was made public, but an additional factor in the union win was political leverage, which, following Sweeney's election, the AFL-CIO was willing to use in support of organizing campaigns. By 1997, MGM had decided to build a casino in Detroit, a historical center of auto unionism, and a place where gambling had recently been legalized. To build a casino there, MGM needed to win one of three gambling licenses, something that HERE and its allies were willing and able to prevent if MGM continued to fight the organizing campaign in Las Vegas. So, finally, the company began to negotiate with Local 226.[52]

Neither of these long and difficult battles would have been

won without both a great deal of support from HERE's national organization and very high levels of rank-and-file militancy. Holding out against intransigent employers and running heavily researched corporate campaigns requires extensive resources. It is estimated that the Frontier campaign alone cost $26 million, and while some of this was raised by the dues increase in Local 226 and some was provided by the AFL-CIO, much was financed by the national union.[53] The national union also sent its best staff organizers and researchers to Las Vegas, including John Wilhelm, who arrived in 1987 and is widely credited with being the architect of the union's success in Las Vegas.

However these resources and staff would not have yielded victories without extensive mobilization from below. Unlike in Los Angeles where the Justice for Janitors staff found a community of immigrants that it was then able to galvanize into action, in Las Vegas HERE organizers had to build a mobilized membership from scratch, without being able to rely on the kind of immigrant networks found in Los Angeles. Drawing on his Yale experience, Wilhelm insured that worker-led committees were formed in every hotel department. Local 226 had traditionally been dominated by bartenders and banquet waiters, an elite (and traditionally White) group of hotel workers, but Wilhelm and his staff insisted on also developing networks of stewards and shop leaders among the poorly paid maids and kitchen helpers, who were largely minority workers. With the growth of the megaresorts, the "back of the house" contingent of the workforce has soared (the MGM hotel, with its 5,005 rooms depends on several hundred chamber maids per shift), and these workers have contributed significantly to the growth of the union as well as to its activist orientation. Also important for building solidarity and leadership is the one-thousand-member City-Wide Organizing Committee, an organization that coordinates rank-and-file union members in systematic efforts to organize the unorganized across the city, and instead of only using paid union "business agents" to settle workers' grievances for them, the local has developed the practice of having workers resolve grievances collectively, mobilizing group actions at the workplace, rather than through bureaucratic paperwork. Experiences with mass arrests and sustained protest actions have served to breed extremely high levels of militancy among hotel workers in Las Vegas who, as one reporter noted, "have plunged into union activity with an abandon not seen since labor's heyday in the 1930s."[54]

Worker militancy and commitment to the practice of "bargaining to organize" have yielded substantial gains in membership. Since 1989 the local's membership has grown from eighteen thousand to nearly fifty thousand today, making it the fastest-growing private-sector local union in the United States. It has substantially improved the living standards of service workers, and Las Vegas is now the only city in America with a decently paid service sector.[55]

Significantly, Local 226 now views itself as a base to strengthen the rest of the labor movement in Las Vegas, suggesting the potential of social movement unionism to regenerate itself and to stimulate broader mobilization. The local has supported organizing campaigns by other unions in hospitals and building trades and has allied itself with local clergymen, many of whom now participate in an interfaith council for worker justice. This group, which in the past often held candlelight vigils in support of Local 226 campaigns, is now particularly active in supporting the United Brotherhood of Carpenters in Las Vegas, which is trying to organize the heavily immigrant workforce of construction workers, partly by exposing abusive practices in the industry and pressuring public institutions not to employ nonunion contractors. Along with a coalition of labor groups, Local 226 published a "Black Book of Nevada Employers" (a play on the "black book of gamblers" that casinos circulate to ban certain gamblers from the casinos), and the interfaith council is planning to open a workers' rights center to educate low-wage workers about their rights and how to organize.[56] Such activities suggest the organizational creativity that is possible where social movement unionism is allowed to take root.

In Las Vegas, Local 226 has gone from being a model of union corruption to becoming an organization that is demonstrating the resurgent potential of the labor movement in the United States. Las Vegas is now widely seen as the "hottest union city in America." It helped to bring John Wilhelm to power in the national union, where he is drawing on Local 226's example to encourage hotel locals in other cities to adopt social movement unionism. Also, as in Los Angeles, the recent history of Las Vegas reveals the power of social movement unionism to be self-expanding. The actions of the hotel workers spurred the clergy to first ally with Local 226 and then to take an active role in organizing other groups of low-wage workers.

Also remarkable is the fact that Las Vegas is a city dominated by the kind of workers—low-paid service workers in the private sector—that many had once assumed were incapable of being organized. Yet a surprisingly strong labor movement has been constructed in that hostile terrain. With all the militancy and social creativity that has been mobilized there in recent years, however, only 15 percent of Las Vegas's private-sector workforce is unionized. From the point of view of the larger national arena, where only 9 percent of the private labor force is unionized, that figure is impressive indeed, but it also shows the degree to which a social movement is constituted as much by the way it is able to represent itself as it is by its numerical size.[57]

CHAPTER FIVE

Two Futures

The recent histories of social movement unionism in Los Angeles and Las Vegas demonstrate the ways in which its practices represent a clear departure from those of postwar business unionism. As such these events hold out the promise and possibility that American unions may at last be able to build a labor movement powerful enough to take on America's virulently antiunion institutions and win. If this were to happen, it would have enormous implications not only for workers in the United States, but, given American's dominant position in the global economy, for workers elsewhere as well.

As it is, union movements across the globe are being forced to respond to new corporate initiatives and are in the process of some reassessment. Even in Europe this is happening. There, where the institutional context is so different (centralized bargaining patterns, the extension of social benefits to all, the rootedness of unions in national political structures), trade unions are struggling to adjust to the new realities of corporate power. For example, in Britain, Prime Minister Blair's uncritical embrace of neoliberalism has generated a strong reaction among the trade unions, organizations that Blair had sought to marginalize. Similarly, Switzerland recently saw its first national labor strike in a generation, an industrial action mobilized by building-construction workers that represented a clear social and psychic disruption for a society that has prided itself on its peacefulness. In Germany, too, trade unions have recently been forced to take a more aggressive stance, one that will likely intensify as the German government and employers continue to chip away at the bedrock of social benefits and employment security to which German workers have been accustomed. And in France, since late 1995 there have emerged new labor organizations, Solidarity, Unity, Democracy (SUD) unions, primarily among schoolteachers and telecommunication and postal workers. These new unions have shown an ability to galvanize the labor movement more generally and have shown they are able to knit together a range of social groups (including the unemployed, immigrants, and high school students) to stand together in the battle to preserve the public system of social provision.

It is important to remember that although their strength has eroded, labor movements are still formidable in European societies, and that the notion of "social partnership" (the term used to characterize labor relations across Europe), while certainly frayed, is still very much intact relative to the United States. At the same time, the pressures of neoliberal reform have placed this arrangement in some jeopardy, at least in the long term. But while the future for labor in Europe may not be entirely clear, the future for American labor is even less so. We see two possibilities: one in which recent efforts to build a new labor movement falter, accelerating the slide toward social dystopia, and one in which these efforts unleash social forces capable of bringing about a more equitable society at home, while hindering efforts to export the American model abroad.

In the first scenario, success stories like Los Angeles and Las Vegas remain isolated cases, labor retreats from movement building, and the percentage of the unionized labor force continues to fall. If this happens, fewer and fewer workers in the United States will have any say over their working lives and only a very small group of highly skilled or strategically placed workers (such as professional athletes, a few highly skilled craftsmen, and some government employees) will remain unionized and thus be able to maintain the kind of social benefits that are granted universally to European citizens. Income differentials will grow beyond their already obscene levels as the equalizing effect of unions is undermined along with union density.

Moreover, if union density continues to decline, the modest political power that labor is able to exercise in the Democratic Party will wither away entirely. Although labor's political influence in the United States is nowhere near the level it is in many other capitalist democracies, there is no question that it is currently one of the few authoritative voices in U.S. society for increased social provision. It is usually the most powerful actor at the national level to push for things like increases in the minimum wage, expansion of health care benefits, and family leave policies. In addition, it is one of the only politically powerful forces in American society that routinely raises a public voice against employers' various "free-trade" schemes and has proved able to marshal enough votes in Congress to defeat some of their most egregious plans. If union density declines precipitously, labor will no longer have the political power to play these roles and progressive political forces will be crippled as a result. Employers will then be able to have their way both at home and abroad, even more so than they do now.

There are several ominous trends that contribute to the likelihood that this scenario will come to fruition, some of which are external to the labor movement and some of which are lodged within labor's own organizations and culture. For one thing, employers remain exceptionally antagonistic to unionization in the United States. America's labor market institutions encourage this stance by rewarding those who successfully fend off unionization. Historically, American employers have proven themselves to be remarkably adept at eventually adjusting to union tactics, and there is evidence that they are once again adapting to the tactics being deployed by the new social movement unionism. At least in California, there are now management consulting firms that specialize in overcoming many of these new tactics, like the practice of card-check recognition and acts of civil disobedience that unions are using in organizing campaigns. And labor law remains solidly weighted toward employers. Moreover, the events of September 11, 2001, have made labor's task even more difficult, largely because it is always hard to organize during periods of political crisis and economic recession, and because the context of severe national emergency has been the pretext for invoking the mantle of national security against unions in an effort to accomplish the long-term Republican Party goal of denying the right of federal employees to join unions.

Soon after September 11, 2001, the Bush administration, which had previously shown an indifference to workers and contempt for their unions, discovered that it could use elements of its international "war against terrorism" to mount a low-intensity war against labor at home. In unveiling his plan for establishing the "Department of Homeland Security," the massive reorganization and consolidation of various existing federal agencies, Bush insisted that all 170,000 workers who would be transferred to the new department should have removed all collective-bargaining rights and civil protections. Several months later, the antilabor timbre of the Bush presidency was amplified when he refused to allow collective-bargaining rights for 56,000 newly federalized airport security screeners.[1]

In the private sector Bush intervened on the side of the shipping companies when they locked out more than ten thousand longshoremen from their jobs at twenty-nine West Coast shipping ports in the autumn of 2002. In the months leading up to the lockout, Bush administration officials had made a series of open threats to union leaders, warning them that any strike or slowdown would be treated as a danger to national security, that the Taft-Hartley Act might be invoked to force a return to work, and that the military might be deployed to replace striking workers on the docks. They further threatened to place the entire waterfront under the legal jurisdiction of the Railway Labor Act, which would have effectively banned waterfront strikes for all time.[2] But perhaps most ominously, the administration advanced a principle elaborated by Defense Secretary Rumsfeld, that in the context of a war on terrorism, all commercial cargo, and not only goods directly intended for military use, shall be considered important to the military. By explicitly conjoining its low-intensity war against labor to the all-encompassing war against terrorism, the Bush administration offered a brief glimpse of the future trajectory for labor in a society where corporate and military interests are interpenetrated and have taken firm hold over the powers of state.

But employer opposition and current government policies are not the only threats to the transformation of the labor movement in the United States. There are serious internal obstacles as well, beginning with the fact that the majority of American unions have yet to adopt the kinds of social movement practices that we have outlined. They have also not committed themselves to making the kind of drastic, systematic changes that it takes to organize nonunionized workers and fight aggressive employer opposition. It is true that there was a sea change at the AFL-CIO when John Sweeney and other new leaders were elected, and the reform forces within the federation have attempted to create a shift in the organizational field to favor reform practices within the affiliated unions. However, these efforts have not yet been enough to spark comprehensive changes throughout the member unions. The voluntary, decentralized nature of the AFL-CIO, supported by the dues of its affiliated national unions and lacking the power to compel national unions to act, makes it so that the federation is unable to make or enforce fundamental changes within any of the affiliated union organizations. The logic of the situation is that the only way to get national unions to change is to persuade them to do so.

The AFL-CIO is certainly trying hard in various ways, including focusing its own resources and programs on organizing, elevating the status of the organizer, prodding affiliated unions to make the kinds of internal changes it takes to be able to organize effectively, and publicizing the successes of unions that have been revitalized by such efforts. But essentially, these tools are not very commanding. Everyone in the labor movement realizes that unions will become less and less powerful, and will gradually die, if they do not organize aggressively; that realization itself represents an enormous shift in the organization. But an inward-looking logic of "servicing the existing membership" still tends to prevail because that is what most union leaders know how to do; it is what facilitated their individual rise to power and what keeps them in office. Sweeney and his allies are clearly hoping that if they can only pile up enough successes, they will leave those who have not adopted the new model with drastically reduced political space and thus force a change (much as they did at the 1995 AFL-CIO convention where they were first elected). Thus far, however, many national union leaders remain recalcitrant. Realistically, only about six of the sixty-five national unions affiliated with the AFL-CIO are engaged in a concerted effort to aggressively organize, and even some of those have yet to put the kind of substantial resources toward organizing that Sweeney and the reform forces are calling for.[3]

It is, after all, wrenching to make the kinds of drastic structural and cultural changes it takes to build a social movement out of an entrenched bureaucratic organization. When unions devote 30 percent or more of their budgets to organizing, as Sweeney and the reformers are strongly pushing them to do, they are forced to devote fewer resources and less staff to servicing, which threatens to leave elected leaders vulnerable to electoral defeat precisely because it is their existing constituency to whom attention to servicing is directed. At the same time, members of most unions in the United States have never gone through any sort of process of preparation to predispose them to experiencing unionism as a social movement, or indeed to experience it as anything other than an occasional series of necessary bureaucratic procedures performed by a designated staff of trade union functionaries, more or less distant from the workplace itself.

Let us be clear. A narrowness of vision is not some natural or intrinsic feature of the American workforce; it is the historically demonstrable product of a political culture that is structured to impose harsh limits on what can be considered reasonable and what can be reasonably considered. For example, only a thoroughly euphemized language of class is permitted in a society that upholds a quasi-official narrative of classlessness while simultaneously permitting truly "exceptional" levels of class inequality (manifested in the severe disparities of wealth concentration, of income, of educational quality, of health care provision, of housing, and of a host of other indices that might be drawn from the social infrastructure of American society). What we have then is a thoroughly "class-full" society that dares not speak its own name. John Sweeney and the union leaders and politicians around him are essentially politically forbidden from even uttering the phrase "the working class," even though it is the principle social object of their attention. Instead, terms like "working families" or "middle-class workers" (or occasionally "the working poor," when pressed) are invoked because they permit one to avoid the specter of class, and therefore to avoid appearing to pose a frontal challenge to the social order itself.

By contrast, the examples of social movement unionism presented above begin to transcend such narrow horizons, in practice creating conditions for a much broader social vision than has been seen in American society for a long time. If an alternative future is at all possible for U.S. labor, and we think that it is, then the experiences in Los Angeles and Las Vegas will not remain isolated cases and will serve as the cornerstone of a social move-ment powerful enough to challenge employers across all sectors of the economy. A fortified labor movement, reconstituted along the lines of the social movement unionism that we see struggling to emerge in various forms, would make an enormous social difference. It would essentially represent the sole institutional counterweight to the American neoliberal juggernaut *within American society itself.*

What are the prospects for the expansion of this movement across the country? Los Angeles and Las Vegas have received a lot of public attention—the first time in recent memory that union actions and the struggles of poor, marginalized workers have been so tightly linked in the mainstream press or the public mind. This attention and the spread of social movement practices in other unions have already begun to have a significant impact in a number of other cities, including very large ones like Atlanta, Boston, Cleveland, Milwaukee, Minneapolis, and Seattle. While perhaps not as dramatic a change as we have seen in Los Angeles and Las Vegas, the fact that the actions of local unions and cen-tral labor councils are generating coordinated activities in a pro-gressive direction is a major departure from the past. So too is the fact that almost one-quarter of the country's roughly six hundred local labor councils—which together represent about half the nation's union members—have registered to become part of the AFL-CIO's "Union Cities" program.[4] This is quite significant because it indicates that these central labor councils want to join the developing social movement, that they want to do things differently, and that they are willing to be shown how. This is not a small thing; it is instead a substantial shift from just a few years ago when central labor councils were the preserve of the most conservative business unions and refused to have anything to do with progressive social groups or questions of fundamental social change.

For example, in one unlikely setting for labor struggle, the possibilities for social unionism have been clearly demonstrated in Stamford, Connecticut. Located in one of the nation's wealthiest counties and home to many corporate executives who commute to New York City as well as to a large number of corporate headquarters, Stamford has had one of the least unionized workforces of all cities on the East Coast. In 1998, the AFL-CIO assembled a multiunion organizing project that within three years had organized and won initial contracts for 4,500 workers. The new contracts not only significantly improved the wages, benefits, and working conditions for health and child care workers, taxi drivers, janitors, and municipal employees, but they also had important social and political effects well beyond the workplace. After conducting systematic analyses of the region's power structure and of workers' needs, the organizing project was persuaded to attempt new forms of mobilization that represented a potentially important strategic departure for the labor movement. Their analyses indicated that a severe lack of affordable housing was a desperate need for workers in the region, so the organizing project developed a sustained campaign with local churches to save and to restore four public housing projects slated for demolition. In the process, the relationships established between African-American churches and the unions became a new source of social power that bolstered the leverage of unions in workplaces throughout the region, that operated to strengthen residential zoning regulations and public-housing protections for low-waged residents, and that elected prolabor African-American and Latino citizens to the Stamford city council.[5]

The Stamford campaign, like those in Los Angeles and Las Vegas, drew together a wide variety of community organizations to support the labor movement. In the unleashing of collective energies and strategic creativity, a broad vision of solidarity suddenly became imaginable in a society where it is normally unthinkable. Similar dynamics are also occurring elsewhere. For example, just when campaigns like Justice for Janitors were beginning to garner widespread attention in the early 1990s, community groups in Baltimore launched an effort to pass a "living-wage" ordinance. Living-wage laws are those that require city contractors (such as agencies that provide social services to poor people, that manage restaurants in city-owned buildings, or that provide supplies for city offices) to pay a so-called living wage, or a wage that enables a full-time worker and his or her family to live at least above the poverty level. (Many private city contractors pay much less, which is one of the main reasons why there was a wave of municipal privatization in the United States in the 1980s.) The idea of the living-wage campaign has proven to be immensely popular at the grassroots level because it offers a moral critique of those who would use public money, directly or indirectly, to create jobs that leave workers and their families in poverty, and because it sets a new standard for corporate accountability outside the public sector. It represents the kind of effort that most union leaders would have disparaged in the past, both because the idea for it came from activists outside the labor movement and because they would have feared that a mandated wage rate might undercut workers' need and support for collective bargaining. In Baltimore, however, the American Federation of State, County, and Municipal Employees (AFSCME), which is one of the unions besides SEIU and HERE that has been actively trying to transform itself, was instrumental in the campaign's success. Since the Baltimore campaign, the living-wage movement, usually allied with progressive local unions, has become the nation's strongest grassroots movement against rising economic inequality, with *more than seventy cities* having passed some form of living-wage legislation.[6]

A shift in the relationship between college students and the labor movement is also underway, as illustrated by a series of events at Harvard University three years ago. It is fitting that the president of Harvard, the noted economist Lawrence Summers, took up his post at the most elite of American universities in the aftermath of a struggle that defied all the econometric models. Several months earlier, in April 2001, Harvard students had engaged in the longest sit-in in the university's history, spending three weeks occupying the office of the former president. They demanded a living wage for Harvard's service workers—the janitors, food servers, and security guards—many of whom were working two and three jobs to support their families. Scores of students occupied the president's office, supported by hundreds outside, while the workers marched in the streets in nightly rallies, their loud chants echoing off the dignified buildings of Harvard Yard. Even some four hundred faculty signed a petition in support of the sit-in and the living-wage campaign. Harvard maintained that it would not negotiate while students remained in the building, but relented when Boston-area unions and AFL-CIO leaders appeared on campus in support of the action. Furthermore, the HERE union local then authorized a strike by its members in support of the action, while making the students honorary members of their union and voting to make academic immunity for the students a prime bargaining point of their own. All together, these acts forced the university to substantially improve wages and workers' rights on campus.[7]

This battle was sociologically significant for several reasons. It occurred at the oldest and most distinguished of the Ivy League universities, an institution whose endowed wealth is greater than that of many multinational corporations. It was a struggle that students initiated on their own, from their contact with service workers at the university, and that conjoined the tactics of the student movement with the immediate concerns *not* of the students themselves, but of a working class that is normally invisible on the academic radar screen. It was essentially the equivalent of another social incongruity: those "Teamsters and Turtles" who came together in Seattle in 1999. Both examples are indicative of an emergent social movement that appears capable of dismantling powerful social barriers. Further glimmers of this were again visible eighteen months later, in October 2002, when a Justice for Janitors strike was launched in Boston and a network of students, former students, clergy, and community leaders mounted daily marches and protests, not stopping until the strike succeeded.[8]

The "anti-sweatshop" campaigns that have emerged on university campuses throughout the United States resemble the living-wage campaigns in their scope and in their ability to awaken a dormant social solidarity. These local campaigns have been mobilized by student activists, including some who were participants in the Union Summer projects that the AFL-CIO had sponsored in the late 1990s. Many others became active without having any links to unions at all. Among the current generation of students, the campaigns have been remarkably successful in raising awareness about corporate exploitation of labor, in creating organizational and interpersonal links between union and student activists, and in allowing students to experience the taste of victory over powerful institutions in the process.

The success of the anti-sweatshop campaign was its ability to combine a broad moral critique with a fairly sophisticated targeting strategy. Universities maintain extremely lucrative royalty arrangements with the suppliers of t-shirts, sweatshirts, and other merchandise bearing the university's logo and name. The suppliers, in turn, engage in subcontracting arrangements with manufacturers, who often rely on cheap "sweat labor" to produce the goods in locations in Asia or wherever labor costs are low. In the United States supplying university clothing and souvenirs is a $2.5 billion industry, and many universities have a substantial financial stake in it (for example, in 1998 one of the largest, the University of Michigan, earned $5.7 million in royalties).[9]

The actions and the public face of a resurgent labor movement have inspired the anti-sweatshop forces, a movement comprised of students, young workers, and university teachers. In the absence of a critique of labor exploitation in the American political lexicon, it is a movement that has become an important vehicle for understanding, criticizing, and mounting a fight against corporate exploitation. Social mobilization in the United States often requires a strong moral critique and vision; for this reason the anti-sweatshop movement has taken hold. Until now, there has been no institutional or political base for furnishing the framework for a critique of the "normal," routine exploitation of workers, but that has become increasingly possible as the anti-sweatshop movement pushes economic practices onto the moral radar screen of middle-class students. Although there has been a long history of student activism in the United States, including the civil rights movement, the movement against the Vietnam War, and the anti-Apartheid struggle, an unambiguous anticorporate politics is only a very recent development among American university students.

One indicator of this movement's success is that it has drawn out from their oak-paneled offices a steady stream of media-connected neoliberal economists who are forced to respond to questions raised by the activists. The anti-sweatshop forces and living-wage proponents, along with all those protesting globalization, have been vilified on the editorial pages of newspapers and on television news programs. Although at first glance this would hardly seem to be an indication of success, for decades in the United States neither leading neoliberal economists nor officially consecrated journalists had to seriously respond to *any issue* that the Left had raised, but now they do.

Another indicator is that the boundaries between groups mobilizing the sorts of actions that we have described and the campaigns to organize unions have become increasingly blurry. That is, staff union organizers are now often loaned to Jobs with Justice coalitions (those groups of union and community organizations responsible for mounting many of the living-wage campaigns), and student activists may have frequent contact with union staff members from UNITE (the clothing workers' union) in the development of anti-sweatshop campaigns. University teachers are now welcomed at meetings of central labor councils, and members of an interfaith religious coalition may work alongside postal workers at a workers' center, providing legal advice to immigrant workers. Such cross-fertilization is entirely new for the postwar American labor movement and is itself indicative of the emergence of a generalized social movement, for it is increasingly a labor movement that is comprised not only of union organizations but of organizations that are decidedly *not* trade unions.

Organizing new unions and new union members, along with activating the space between unions, will be crucial in rebuilding the labor movement as a social movement. The examples of social unionism that we know about suggest that new spaces have begun to open up—and new organizations to form—in which workers, immigrants, and peace activists of differing racial and ethnic backgrounds now come together and interact. As a result there exists, for the first time in many decades, possibilities for new social visions to be enacted, to be lived.

Although we do not feel at all compelled to conclude on an optimistic note, we can reasonably say that however weak its relational position may be, "labor" has begun to conjure up an entirely different vision, as a constellation of groups, institutions, and movements that are viewed as dealing in a central way with matters of social justice. Does this mean that labor will be able to overcome the formidable obstacles to achieving significant social power in American society? That is still very much an open question, but for the first time in a long time it may very well be possible.

NOTES

PREFACE

1. Schiffrin, *Business of Books*, p. 145.

CHAPTER 1: WHY LABOR MATTERS

1. The boasts have continued even during the recent economic slow-down. In the magazine section of the *New York Times* on October 27, 2002, M. Lewis reported that "employment in the 100 boom-era companies climbed 26 percent" from the end of 1999 to the end of 2001. "That's 177,000 jobs," he exclaimed (see M. Lewis, "In Defense of the Boom," p. 60).

2. One of America's leading economists, Paul Krugman, points out that "most Americans assume that because we are the richest country in the world, with real GDP per capita higher than that of most other major advanced countries, Americans must be better off across the board—that it's not just our rich who are richer than their counterparts abroad, but that the typical American family is much better off than the typical family elsewhere, and that even our poor are well off by foreign

standards. But that's not true." When things like heath care, child care, work hours per year, and so on are included in our measure of living standards, this is even less true (see Krugman, "For Richer"). This inequality in living standards has especially harmful effects on American children. As Lee Rainwater and Timothy Smeeding show in their careful analysis of living standards in rich democracies, there are more children (both proportionately and absolutely) who live in low-income households in the United States than in any other rich democracy. Moreover, these children are worse off than low-income children in every other advanced industrial country, except the United Kingdom. The average low-income child in the eleven European counties the authors studied was at least 25 percent better off than the average low-income child in the United States. And this figure almost certainly understates the level of deprivation of American low-income children, for it does not take into account things like unequal access to health care, childcare, and education. At the other end of the social universe, American children of high-income families are *much* better off than kids in other OECD countries (Rainwater and Smeeding, "Comparing Living Standards Across Nations"; Smeeding, "No Child Left Behind?").

3. During its boom years in the 1990s the information technology sector in the United States generated jobs at a substantially faster rate than other industries, but still contributed a small share (7.5 percent of all new jobs) to total job growth. In 1999, information technology occupations made up only 2 percent of all employment (up from 1.3 percent in 1989), and workers in these jobs fared no better than workers with comparable education and experience in other kinds of jobs (Mishel, Bernstein, and Schmitt, *State of Working America 2000–2001*, p. 2).

4. Founder and CEO of Amazon.com Jeffrey Bezos became fabulously wealthy, owning $7.5 billion in stock holdings. Stock options recently paid to three of his top executives at the firm were worth $1.3 billion, $744 million, and $207 million, respectively. Meanwhile, customer service representatives are paid 10 dollars per hour upon hiring (equivalent to $20,000 per year), with a chance to earn stock options; however, only 30–50 percent of these employees stay on the job long enough to meet the one-year eligibility. In any event, it is doubtful that

many workers would be able to afford stock options on $20,000 a year, as the living wage for a family of one adult and two children was recently estimated to be $30,000 a year, which amounts to $14 an hour. See Leibovich, "Service Without a Smile"; Strauss, "Billionaires Club"; and Ehrenreich, *Nickel and Dimed.*

5. Lang, "Behind the Prosperity"; Greenhouse, "Janitors Struggle at the Edges."

6. For a compelling account of temporary workers toiling alongside permanent workers, see Smith, *Crossing the Great Divide*, ch. 4.

7. Microsoft recently agreed to pay $97 million to settle an eight-year-old lawsuit in which thousands of "temporary" employees successfully argued that they were illegally denied benefits by the company (Greenhouse, "Temp Workers at Microsoft Win Lawsuit"). There are more than six thousand temporary workers among the twenty-five thousand or so Microsoft employees in the United States, virtually none of whom are represented by a union (Greenhouse, "Unions Need Not Apply"). Amazon and Microsoft both have gradually begun "outsourcing" their customer service work to New Delhi, India, where skilled customer service positions pay less than 10 percent of the wages paid in Seattle (Greenhouse, "Unions Pushing to Organize Thousands"; Jackson, "Newswatch").

8. The original "bracero program" in the 1940s and 1950s allowed California agricultural employers to hire Mexican citizens to work on temporary contracts at very low wages and under harsh conditions in fruit and vegetable fields. The threat of deportation was routinely used as a stick to ward off collective action. In addition to the recent H1-B visas for software developers and computer programmers (many of whom will be recruited from India, China, and the Philippines), agricultural and meat-packing interests are also seeking a return to the bracero program as a way of recruiting low-wage labor for their industries (see Bacon, "Immigrants Find High-Tech Servitude"; Enrich, "High-Tech Cheap Labor").

9. Greenhouse, "Unions Pushing to Organize Thousands"; Greenhouse, "Amazon.com Is Using the Web."

10. See Fischer et al., *Inequality by Design*, p. 138, for a discussion of some of the ways in which Americans are aided by the larger society but

imagine that their achievements have come through individual efforts alone.

11. See Royster, *Race and the Invisible Hand;* Wilson, *When Work Disappears;* Granovetter, *Getting a Job.*

12. Lynch, "Payoffs to Alternative Training," p. 63.

13. R. B. Freeman, "How Labor Fares," p. 19; see also Freeman and Katz, *Differences and Changes.*

14. Fischer et al., "Myths about Inequality in America."

15. Mishel, Bernstein, and Boushey, *State of Working America 2002– 2003*, p. 427.

16. These six occupations are: retail salespersons; cashiers; personal care home health aides; teacher assistants; janitors and cleaners (including maids); and nurse's aides, orderlies, and attendants (see Frey, Abresch, and Yeasting, *America by the Numbers*, p. 113).

17. Quoted in Tilly, *Half a Job*, p. 47.

18. In the case of Wal-Mart, it is important to point out that we are talking about the hours of work that Wal-Mart actually pays for, which is not necessarily the total number of hours actually worked. Workers have filed class-action and individual lawsuits in twenty-nine states alleging that Wal-Mart forced them to work "off the clock" in order to meet profit targets (see Greenhouse, "Suits Say Wal-Mart Forces Workers"; Tower, "Sam's Dream").

19. Klein, *No Logo*, p. 476.

20. Mishel, Bernstein, and Schmitt, *State of Working America 2000– 2001*, pp. 243–53.

21. Mishel, Bernstein, and Boushey, *State of Working America 2002– 2003*, p. 429.

22. See Wacquant, *Les Prisons De La Misere*, p. 90; see also Western and Beckett, "How Unregulated Is the US Labor Market?"

23. Although youth unemployment has been unusually intractable throughout Western Europe relative to the United States, a respected British economist has told the *Financial Times* that "between 1988 and 1994, *11 per cent* of men aged 25–55 were not in work in France, com-

pared with 13 per cent in the UK, *14 per cent in the US*, and 15 per cent in Germany" (quoted in Gray, *False Dawn*, p. 113; emphasis added).

24. See Mishel, Bernstein, and Schmitt, *State of Working America 2000–2001*, p. 120; and Fischer et al. *Inequality by Design*, pp. 111–15.

25. All male blue-collar workers saw sizeable declines in hourly wages between 1973 and 2001(even when we include the wage growth that occurred between 1995 and 2001!). So, too, did most male service workers. (An exception is those employed in protective services, who earned 32 cents more an hour than they had in 1973.) Although women's wages rose steadily across all these occupational categories, this is largely because they lagged so far behind the wages of men prior to 1973, and their wages continue to be substantially lower than those of men in the same occupational categories. See Mishel, Bernstein, and Boushey, *State of Working America 2002–2003*, pp. 125–26.

26. Ibid., pp. 131–41; Mishel, Bernstein, and Schmitt, *State of Working America 2000–2001*, pp. 129–37. A "poverty-level wage" is designated by "the hourly wage that a full-time, year-round worker must earn to sustain a family of four at the poverty threshold," or $8.70 in the year 2001. Although the official "poverty threshold" is a precise figure that carries great authority, the computational model from which it is derived is widely regarded as arbitrary and outdated, essentially understating by half the percent of the population that actually lives under conditions of material deprivation.

27. Mishel, Bernstein, and Boushey, *State of Working America 2002–2003*, pp. 161, 163.

28. Ibid., pp. 159–60. Those with some college education saw a very modest 1.5 percent real wage gain in the period between 1973 and 2001; those with a college degree experienced a 16 percent real wage increase; those with an advanced degree enjoyed a 19 percent boost.

29. The figure on compensation for leading CEOs is for 2001 and is from Klinger et al., *Executive Excess 2002;* and Lavelle, "Executive Pay." Salary, bonuses, and stock options exercised are included in the figure, but unexercised stock options are not. The ratio of CEO to average

worker pay is from Mishel, Bernstein, and Boushey, *State of Working America 2002–2003*, p. 215.

30. For figures on CEO compensation in France and Germany, see *Business Week, International Editions*, August 9, 1999, p. 24; and Mishel, Bernstein, and Boushey, *State of Working America 2002–2003*, pp. 213–15.

31. See Wolff, "Recent Trends in Wealth Ownership, 1983–1988"; Wolff, *Top Heavy*.

32. Statistics cited in Mishel, Bernstein, and Boushey, *State of Working America 2002–2003*, pp. 143–47.

33. For example, of those in the lowest fifth of wage earners, of whom only 33.4 percent receive any employer-provided health insurance, there was a 7.3 percent decline between 1979 and 2000, which is also the period in which pension coverage was reduced by a rate of 1.5 percent (only *18 percent* of low-wage workers receive employer-provided pensions). Generally, for workers within the bottom two-fifths of wage earners, the costs of purchasing health care coverage for themselves and their families and of investing in a private pension plan are prohibitively expensive. It is among this group that the national estimate of forty-four million uninsured Americans is overwhelmingly drawn. Figures are cited in Mishel, Bernstein, and Schmitt, *State of Working America 2000–2001*, pp. 137–40.

34. For a discussion of comparative life expectancy statistics, see Krugman, "For Richer."

35. This has not always been the case. Thirty years ago Americans worked *fewer* hours per year than either the French or the Germans, according to R. B. Freeman, "How Labor Fares," p. 3.

36. Mishel, Bernstein, and Boushey, *State of Working America 2002–2003*, pp. 423, 425. Sweden has also shown an increase in the average annual hours worked between 1979 and 2000, but the increase has only brought Sweden's average to 1,624 hours per year, which is fifth from the bottom on the list of OECD countries. The United States was twentieth, with 1,877 hours. The broad implications of overwork in the United States are examined in Schor, *Overworked American*.

37. Mishel, Bernstein, and Schmitt, *State of Working America 2000–*

2001, p. 401. Also see Schor, *Overworked American*. Obviously, since sixteen represents the *average* number of annual paid vacation days in the United States, a great many workers receive less, and some receive no annual paid vacation. Moreover, there are only eight to ten paid holidays for U.S. workers, while the mean number across Europe is twelve, according to R. B. Freeman, "How Labor Fares," p. 22.

38. See the aptly titled book by Linder and Nygaard, *Void Where Prohibited: Rest Breaks and the Right to Urinate on Company Time*, pp. 1, 9. They present data (p. 174) indicating that one-third of workers employed in medium or large establishments (and approximately 50 percent of those working for small establishments or for the government) do not receive paid rest periods.

39. In addition, while unemployment insurance covers American workers at 50 percent of their pay for six months, workers in Europe normally receive sixteen months of unemployment coverage at 47 percent of their pay according to R. B. Freeman, "How Labor Fares," p. 22. There is no mandated provision with regard to severance pay in the United States.

40. Sometimes social benefits are offered as an indirect effect of union efforts. As Jacoby documents in *Modern Manors*, some large nonunion corporations like IBM and Eastman Kodak set up "welfare capitalism" as a way of ensuring that their workplaces will remain "union free."

41. Abraham and Houseman discuss the differences between German and American labor market policies with regard to layoffs in "Job Security in America."

42. "For Greenspan, Ease in Firing Is a U.S. Plus," p. 1.

43. Ackerman, "Supply-Side Journalism"; also see Blank, "Does a Larger Social Safety Net Mean Less Economic Flexibility?"

44. Russakoff, "When Pay Can't Cover Childcare."

45. According to a survey conducted by the Children's Defense Fund, the average amount that an American parent pays for child care for two children, that are, say, three and four years old, is about $900 per month, but in many places parents are forced to pay as much as $1,200 or more (see Helburn and Bergmann, *America's Childcare*, p. 20).

46. Bergmann, *Saving Our Children;* Wacquant, *Urban Outcasts;* Wacquant, "Comparative Structure and Experience."

47. To be clear, one should not romanticize European societies, all of which are experiencing ongoing political battles to reduce social provisions. We compare Europe with America in this chapter because it is so often held up as a negative example, and because even while the welfare state is under attack there, most European societies have held onto universal social provision as a principal.

48. R. B. Freeman, "How Labor Fares," p. 19; Blau and Kahn, "International Differences in Male Wage."

49. Ozaki, *Negotiating Flexibility,* p. 146.

50. As we will discuss in Chapter 4, unions have recently begun to find ways around this election system because employers have been so effective in manipulating it to their advantage.

51. See Fantasia, *Cultures of Solidarity.*

52. The effectiveness of this symbolic "disappearing act" is evident when, for example, consumers are faced with the threat of an airline strike and the popular media accords great weight and attention to the "inconveniences" and the "disruptions" visited on the "traveling public," while mostly ignoring or downplaying injustices in the experience of airline workers within a deregulated industry.

53. The systematic dissolution of worker rights in the United States is documented in Fantasia, "Dictature sur le proletariat"; see also the report issued by the organization, Human Rights Watch, entitled *Unfair Advantage: Worker's Freedom of Association in the U.S.*

54. Greenhouse, "Trying to Overcome Embarrassment"; Ernsberger Jr., "Wal-Mart World."

55. See Kaufman, "As Biggest Business." For an analysis of the Wal-Mart empire, see Ortega, *In Sam We Trust;* and Vance and Scott, *Wal-Mart.*

56. This intense pressure to consume has no doubt contributed to the serious crisis involving the savings rate, which has declined from about 8 percent in 1980, to 4 percent in the early 1990s, to the current level of *zero*. According to Schor in *Do Americans Shop Too Much?,*

"About 2/3 of American households do not save in a typical year" (pp. 10–11). Meanwhile, credit card debt has soared as unpaid balances currently average $7,000 per household, with the typical household paying $1,000 annually in interest and penalties, and annual bankruptcy rates having risen from 200,000 in 1980 to 1.4 million in 1998.

57. In 1998 only 19.2 percent of Americans had *direct* stock holdings (shares bought in a particular company); while 43.4 percent of Americans had *indirect* stock holdings (shares bought through mutual funds or held in pension funds) and slightly more than one-third of households (36.3 percent) held stock worth more than $5,000 (directly or indirectly). See Mishel, Bernstein, and Schmitt, *State of Working America 2000–2001*, pp. 266–67.

58. Bourdieu, "Social Space and the Genesis of 'Classes'"; Fantasia, "Myth of the Labor Movement."

CHAPTER 2: AN EXCEPTIONALLY HOSTILE TERRAIN

1. Voss, *Making of American Exceptionalism*, ch. 2.

2. Translated by Patricia M. Hocking and C. T. Husbands.

3. The literature on American exceptionalism is voluminous. An excellent recent statement and an extensive bibliography can be found in Lipset and Marks, *It Didn't Happen Here*. Karabel offers a helpful review of earlier scholarship in "Failure of American Socialism Reconsidered"; and Gerber provides a very useful overview of the more recent literature in "Shifting Perspectives on American Exceptionalism."

4. Voss, *Making of American Exceptionalism*, chs. 7–8.

5. See ibid., p. 226. With such enormous resources and strategic leverage pitted against them, the Knights were forced to appeal to small employers, a historically specific strategy of populism that drew on the ideology of working-class republicanism and led to internal divisions that rent the organization apart. Thus, ideology and solidarity may have appeared to be the key factors in the demise of the Knights, but the

overwhelming force that shaped the range of available choices was employer mobilization.

6. In France, as Friedman points out, the state feared that any unrest might precipitate a constitutional crisis. Especially when strikes involved large numbers of workers (as Knights' strikes typically did), the state tended to intervene. Intervention generally resulted in shorter strikes and employer concessions (see Friedman, "State and the Making of the Working Class"). In England, although the British state generally maintained a "studied appearance of neutrality" in labor disputes, it usually worked behind the scenes to encourage mediation and conciliation (see Holt, "Trade Unionism"; Fox, *History and Heritage;* and Jacoby, *Masters to Managers*).

7. Archer details the increasing use of state repression against American workers—and especially American workers who were involved with inclusive unions—in the late nineteenth century. He compares repression in the United States to repression in Australia and finds that both in terms of the number and types of soldiers and police deployed, and in terms of what they did once they were deployed, repression was greater in the United States. Moreover, he documents close ties between major employers and federal and state militias in the United States (see Archer, "Does Repression Help Create Labor Parties?"; statistics cited can be found on pp. 193, 199). See also Mann, *Sources of Social Power,* 2:635, for a comparison of the number of workers killed in industrial disputes from 1871–1914 in Western Europe and the United States: seven in England; thirty-five in France; sixteen in Germany, and between five and eight hundred in the United States!

8. Gordon, Edwards, and Reich, *Segmented Work, Divided Workers,* pp. 141–43.

9. Warner, *Streetcar Suburbs,* pp. 242–43.

10. A comparative study of the experience of two towns in Massachusetts indicates that where industrial unionism had deep roots, working-class institutions assimilated immigrants, thus strengthening community-wide solidarity. And where there were fewer such integrating institutions, immigrants formed tightly knit ethnic enclaves that

undermined collective action and wider community solidarity (see Cumbler, *Working Class Community*).

11. When forced as a matter of organizational efficiency, Gompers occasionally encouraged the organization of Black workers or the creation of local organizations of women workers, but generally both he and the leaders of most craft unions explicitly excluded Blacks and women from their ranks, as well as those without a proper "trade." Furthermore, both the AFL and its affiliated unions mobilized strenuously to support the exclusion of Chinese immigrants, an effort that was enhanced by a vicious xenophobia (see the chapter entitled "Samuel Gompers and Business Unionism" in Buhle, *Taking Care of Business*).

12. Ibid., p. 66.

13. See Rothenbuhler, "Liminal Fight."

14. See Fantasia, *Cultures of Solidarity*, pp. 39–44.

15. Statistics are quoted from Lichtenstein, *State of the Union*, pp. 52–53.

16. For a sketch of the political and cultural coloration of the CIO, see Cohen, *Making a New Deal*; and Zieger, *CIO*.

17. Fantasia, *Cultures of Solidarity*, pp. 46–47.

18. From September 1936 through May 1937, some 485,000 workers engaged in sit-down strikes, closing plants that employed 600,000 other workers (see Boyer and Morais, *Labor's Untold Story*).

19. See Brecher, *Strike!*, ch. 5; Fantasia, *Cultures of Solidarity*, pp. 46–47.

20. Archer, "Does Repression Help Create Labor Parties?" pp. 217–18; Lichtenstein, *State of the Union*, pp. 50–53; Brecher, *Strike!*, pp. 204–35.

21. Fantasia, *Cultures of Solidarity*, p. 46; Lichtenstein, *State of the Union*, p. 51.

22. Amenta and Skocpol compare the influence of American and British labor in the mobilization of the war effort in "Redefining the New Deal," pp. 113–19.

23. Support came from the Communist Party as well, for as its line shifted in response to the breakdown of the Hitler-Stalin pact, its trade

union members and supporters (still very influential in many CIO unions) suddenly became staunch defenders of the no-strike pledge. Harry Bridges, the militant head of the West Coast longshoremen, and a well-known communist, went so far as to advise workers that "your unions today must become instruments of speedup of the working class of America" (see Cochran, *Labor and Communism,* pp. 206, 214).

24. Scott and Homans, "Reflections on the Wildcat Strikes." Most unions never polled their members' views on the no-strike policy, but the United Automobile Workers did in 1944, and 65 percent of those voting upheld the no-strike pledge, while *during the same period* a majority of auto workers were engaging in wildcat strikes. Such violations were justified by workers in response to the industrial immorality of war production and to the tripartite collaboration (of business, labor, and government leaders) that made it possible. Glaberman analyzed the situation in his *Wartime Strikes.*

25. Statistics compiled by the Bureau of Labor Statistics for the period showed that there were 88,100 workers killed and 11,112,600 injured in production accidents at home, compared to 1,058,000 war casualties, according to Boyer and Morais, *Labor's Untold Story,* p. 336.

26. See chapter entitled "The Bureaucratic Imperative," in Lichtenstein, *Labor's War at Home.*

27. Jacoby, "American Exceptionalism Revisited"; Vogel, "Why Businessmen Distrust Their State."

28. A postwar study of six industries revealed widespread management concern over the loss of control in the plants, with one automobile industry executive declaring, "If any manager in this industry tells you he has control of his plant he is a damn liar" (Chamberlain, *Union Challenge,* p. 41). Brody reported that at the beginning of the postwar period "rank and file militancy commonly elevated the shop steward to co-equal status" with shop-floor management (Brody, *Workers in Industrial America,* pp. 180–81).

29. "McCarthyism" was named for Senator Joseph McCarthy, a senator from Wisconsin and a leader of the anticommunist crusade in Congress. For good overviews of various aspects of postwar American

anticommunism and the labor movement, see Griffith and Theoharis, *Specter*; Cochran, *Labor and Communism*; and Sexton, *War on Labor*.

30. Prior to Taft-Hartley, the NLRB sometimes used card-checks to ascertain that a majority of workers wanted a union. After Taft-Hartley, the NLRB would not on its own accept card-check recognition. In recent years, as we will discuss in Chapter 4, unions have begun to find ways to circumvent the NLRB election system, one of which is to pressure employers to accept card-check recognition. The difference is that today unions must convince *employers* to accept card-checks; prior to Taft-Hartley, the unions had only to convince a sympathetic NLRB. For a good analysis of how the NLRB operated in its early years, see Brody, "Labor Elections."

31. Recall that in the United States trade unions are only constituted within specific workplaces or enterprises, rather than on a national or industry-wide basis. A "closed shop" was an agreement between an employer and a union that, as a condition of employment, all employees must belong to the union before being hired. The employer thus agreed to retain only union members in his or her business. The "closed shop," outlawed by the Taft-Hartley Act, was superceded by the "union shop" arrangement, in which the employer is free to hire anyone he or she chooses, but once a union has been certified, all workers must become members within a specified period of time after being hired and continue their union membership as a condition of continuing employment. Changes instituted under the Taft-Hartley Act thus shifted the control over local labor markets, and the principles governing that control, from the union to the employer.

32. In recent years, several European automakers have chosen to locate their manufacturing operations in the South in the hopes of avoiding unionization, even while maintaining relations with their unions back home. For example, in 1994 Daimler Benz (now "Daimler Chrysler") located its first American-based Mercedes plant in a rural section of Alabama, a "right-to-work" state with a unionization rate of just 9.7 percent, compared to a rate of 21 percent in Michigan, the traditional heart of the automobile industry. Wages and benefits at the

Alabama plant were far less than in the company's German factories, but executives soon decided that steady wage increases might ward off unionization attempts. By 1999 the wages were comparable to those of German autoworkers, but the benefits paid were much less and many fewer, and the company has been able to operate without having to negotiate with anything equivalent to the powerful German trade union, IG Metall (see Meredith, "Union March on Alabama").

33. Sympathy strikes and secondary boycotts were actions organized by workers who were not directly involved in a labor dispute to support those workers who were. Social movements, like the civil rights movement and the anti-Apartheid movement are contemporary examples of the power of such tactics. By banning such actions, Taft-Hartley effectively declared interunion solidarity illegal, and by allowing the president to temporarily halt strikes, a potent administrative mechanism was provided to break the momentum of the strike mobilization process, reducing any benefits that unions might gain from the timing of strikes. Within the first year of the law's passage the presidential injunction was used to halt seven strikes, and during the next two decades it was invoked in twenty-two cases.

34. The social distance between the union leadership and the rank and file had grown during the war years, as union leaders were brought into the tripartite supervision of war production (along with industry and military leaders) via the National War Labor Board. In the context of war emergency, labor leaders were "called to Washington" for consultation, were expected to dampen worker militancy by upholding the wartime no-strike pledge, and, consequently, were generally accorded a level of legitimacy and respectability that they had not known previously. Hence, as the war ended, the new figure of the "labor statesman" was increasingly common in policymaking circles in Washington, D.C. (see Lichtenstein, *Labor's War at Home*; and Mills, *New Men of Power*).

35. Stepan-Norris and Zeitlin, *Left Out*.

36. Stevens, "Blurring the Boundaries"; Weir, *Politics and Jobs*; Lichtenstein, *Walter Reuther*, especially pp. 287–98.

37. Stability was enhanced by Taft-Hartley in a provision through

which union dues would be automatically deducted from the union member's paycheck, with the collected dues delivered directly by the employer to the trade union. This ensured a degree of membership stability and saved the unions from having to repeatedly collect dues from each individual member, a costly and time-consuming activity (and one that would have required a steady level of membership satisfaction with union representation!).

38. While Bell explicitly advanced this view in *The End of Ideology*, Riesman *(The Lonely Crowd)* and Whyte Jr. *(The Organization Man)* contributed to it in an implicit way by their focus on the plight of the individual in mass organizations, a perspective that helped supplant questions of class conflict and domination.

39. Although the poverty rate hovered around 25 percent of the population after the war, poverty was basically nonexistent as a public issue until the early 1960s, when the publication of Harrington's *The Other America* began to have an impact on public discourse. Just as influential was the broadcast of *Harvest of Shame*, a historic television documentary that exposed the conditions of migrant farmworkers in the United States.

40. Although the number of wildcat strikes in the United States is impossible to quantify with any precision, rough estimates suggest that the number may have exceeded the number of official strikes, so that contrary to the expectations of the "mature industrialism thesis," spontaneous, unofficial, and illegal forms of industrial action may have actually preponderated through much of the postwar period. For a more detailed discussion of the wildcat strike phenomenon, see Fantasia and Stepan-Norris, "Labor in Action."

41. One management commentator estimated that between 1963 and 1972, the number of filed written grievances doubled from 138,000 to 264,000 (cited in Fantasia, *Cultures of Solidarity*, pp. 62–63). A rare look at the grievance-resolution process from the perspective of the rank-and-file worker is by Spencer, a former steelworker, in a chapter entitled "Five Steps to Failure," included in his *Blue Collar*.

42. Bell's view, advanced in a paper that he first presented to Georges

Friedmann's seminar at the Sorbonne, was that American unionism existed "in two contexts, as a *social movement* and as an economic force *(market unionism)*." This might have been a reasonable perspective except that for Bell the former was solely constituted by the pragmatic ideology of "laborism," thereby effectively eliminating *on paper* the communist participation and labor radicalism that had already been eliminated institutionally in the rather brutal anticommunist purges (see Bell, "Capitalism of the Proletariat," pp. 211–26).

43. During the same period, hourly earnings for coal miners rose 80 percent, for steelworkers 102 percent, for auto workers 88 percent, and for meatpackers 114 percent. Figures cited in Moody, *Injury to All*, p. 65. In contrast to Europe, as Freeman has noted, where wages are more or less centrally determined at a national level, and where the terms of collective bargaining between unions and employer federations may be extended to all workers in a given industry, in the U.S. wage setting is a highly decentralized and uncoordinated process by which tens of thousands of nonunion firms set wage rates (R. B. Freeman, *Working Under Different Rules*, pp. 18–20). Until the mid-1970s, national patterns of wages and working conditions were negotiated between top labor leaders and top executives of the firms, but today those patterns have been weakened and most union contracts are negotiated by local labor leaders on a company-by-company and plant-by-plant basis.

44. By 1970 installment debt in the United States was $100 billion annually (by 1975 it reached nearly $165 billion and by 1979, $307 billion annually). It suggests that those large consumer durable goods that served as material symbols of American working-class affluence for two generations of academics and conservatives were goods purchased on "easy credit terms" and actually represented debt obligations and depreciating assets rather than an accretion of household wealth (Green, *World of the Worker*, p. 215; see also Sexton and Sexton, "Myth of Affluence").

45. Quoted in Slaughter, *Concessions and How to Beat Them*, p. 7.

46. A general survey of the contract negotiations conducted during the 1980–83 recession is provided in ibid., pp. 14–25.

47. Union "decertification" refers to a legal provision of the Taft-

Hartley Act through which unions can be stripped of their legal standing. In the United States, strikes by federal employees (as opposed to government workers employed at the state, county, or municipal level) are banned, which provided Reagan with the legal justification for firing the PATCO strikers (and which occurred at the same time as Reagan was enthusiastically cheering for that other "illegal" strike by "public employees," mobilized by Poland's *Solidarnosc).*

48. Like many people, it seems that the leader of PATCO, Robert Poli, was thoroughly beguiled by "the great communicator," Ronald Reagan. Prior to the strike, while openly expressing sympathy with the controllers (in exchange for their electoral support) Reagan's Department of Transportation employed a notorious union-busting law firm to oversee the coming contract negotiations with the air traffic controllers, and five months before the strike the Federal Aviation Administration under Reagan appointed the antiunion head of an aircraft company as its administrator (see Hurd, "Retrospective on the PATCO Strategy," Appendix I, p. 206).

49. In 1965 the top executives of many of the largest corporations (including AT&T, General Motors, Union Carbide, U.S. Steel, General Dynamics, General Electric, Exxon, International Harvester, B.F. Goodrich, and so on) came together to form the "Labor Law Study Group" to begin to develop and implement a wide-ranging antiunion agenda. This organization later became known as the "Business Roundtable," and by the early 1980s it had successfully mobilized political action in Washington against trade unionism together with a wider group of industry "trade organizations" (the "Council on a Union-Free Environment" of the National Association of Manufacturers, the Associated Builders and Contractors, the National Hospital Association, the National Retail Merchants Association, and so on) who were actively providing direct assistance to employers seeking to rid their companies of unions (see Fantasia, "Assault on American Labor"; Moody, *Injury to All,* p. 128).

50. *Fortune* magazine, bellwether of corporate thinking, published a lead article in its November 1981 edition entitled "The Decline of

Strikes," which celebrated "the new, increasingly militant tactics of management" and concluded with a portentous call to arms: "Managers are discovering that strikes can be broken, that the cost of breaking them is often lower than the cost of taking them, and that strikebreaking (assuming it to be legal and nonviolent) doesn't have to be a dirty word. In the long run, this new perception by business could turn out to be big news, not only about labor relations but about the health of the U.S. economy."

51. Incredibly, in the United States workers have the putative "right to strike," at the same time as employers are able to hire *permanent* replacement workers to effectively nullify that right. Moreover, strikers are severely constrained from preventing their "replacements" from taking their jobs. Normally, at even the first *hint* of physical "violence" against strikebreakers (easily manufactured if it doesn't occur "naturally") the employer will move quickly to secure a legal injunction against mass picket lines, almost invariably granted by a local judge, which limits the number of pickets to six or fewer at each entrance to the building. The power of collective action is thus immediately drained of its potential, another legacy of the 1947 Taft-Hartley Act.

52. The study, commissioned by the U.S. government's General Accounting Office, was published by Schnell and Gramm, "Empirical Relations."

53. Although large corporations could rely on their own legal departments, smaller companies were the main market for antiunion legal consultants who assisted plant-level managers in navigating their way through the labor laws. These lawyers and consultants invariably worked behind the scenes, advising companies as they proceeded through the sorts of procedures outlined above. Other companies were formed to supply not only the logistical resources for strikebreaking but also the strikebreakers themselves, while the more notorious security firms specializing in "strike situations" (like the Wackenhut Corporation) operated like military units, erecting barbed-wire fencing and using guard dogs, surveillance equipment, and armed guards to establish

a "secure perimeter" around a strike-bound plant. Detailed strikebreaking contingency plans were readily available to employers in publications with titles such as "When Labor Troubles Strike: An Action Handbook" and "Operating During Strikes."

54. In other words, once the "social contract" was irrevocably broken workers revealed themselves to be no longer very "exceptional" after all; in fact, it has mostly been *employers* in the United States who have enjoyed a truly *exceptional* existence relative to their European counterparts. Some studies of particular American strikes in this period are Rachleff, *Hard Pressed in the Heartland*, Rosenblum, *Copper Crucible*; Brecher, *Strike!*; Kingsolver, *Holding the Line*; and Fantasia, *Cultures of Solidarity*. See also Juravitch and Bronfenbrenner, *Ravenswood*, a study of the lockout of workers belonging to the United Steelworkers at Ravenswood Aluminum in West Virginia in the early 1990s. This lockout, like the other examples listed here, involved replacement workers, but unlike the other examples, it resulted in an important union victory.

55. The penalty against employers for illegally firing union activists is typically a back-pay settlement, without any additional fine. Most unfair labor practice charges against employers are eventually upheld by the National Labor Relations Board, and while the numbers appear to drop after 1980, the drop actually represented a decline in the number of union-representation elections that were held. That is, since the number of elections fell by more than 50 percent in 1981 and the rate of unfair labor practices declined by much less, employer antiunionism can be seen to have become *more* significant in the elections held after 1980. The number of representation elections declined largely because antiunion lawyers and consultants increasingly encouraged employers to be more aggressive in the early stages of union campaigns, thus derailing the process before elections could be held (and the NLRB under Ronald Reagan often acted on behalf of employers by delaying elections, giving employers additional time to obstruct the election process).

56. The U.S. government calls on other countries to respect a worker's right to association as a bedrock principal of a democratic soci-

ety, but these rights are denied at home when American employers treat unionization as a financial consideration instead of as an issue of human rights. So concluded a 2000 report by Human Rights Watch, which documents widespread violations of American workers' right to organize. See Roth, "Unfair Advantage."

57. In one seminar for corporate executives arranged by an antiunion consulting firm, the lecturer emphasized the value of delaying tactics in disrupting the union campaign: "Delay is crucial to your strategy. Delay in setting up a first conference. Dig up issues on appropriate units, supervisors, confidential employees, part-time workers. Don't consent to an election until all issues are resolved. Then delay hearings. Delay briefs with excuses. Stall and delay wherever possible. When 30 percent of employees have signed cards the union can file for an election. Can you stack the election? Yes—hire new people. Time is on the side of the employer" (quoted in Georgine, "From Brass Knuckles to Briefcases," p. 96).

58. Kochan, Katz, and McKersie, *Transformation of American Industrial Relations*, pp. 242–45; Kassarda, "Industrial Restructuring and the Changing Location of Jobs."

59. Dark, *Unions and the Democrats*, p. 16.

60. The public-sector union rate is much higher—37 percent of the labor force—and it has actually risen in the past two decades. The key difference between the two has to do with private- versus public-sector *employers*. Government managers are subject to immediate local and state political pressure and therefore have been much more reluctant to engage in open and violent forms of union busting, compared to corporate employers in the private sector. In this sense, the sort of aggression that President Reagan unleashed against PATCO in 1981 was uncharacteristic of labor relations in the public sector. Although union membership rates are certainly not the only important measure of labor's power, they do represent the "bottom line" with respect to labor's institutional presence in an enterprise, in an industry, and in the economy.

CHAPTER 3: BUREAUCRATS, "STRONGMEN," MILITANTS, AND INTELLECTUALS

1. Moody, "On Eve of Seattle Trade Protests."

2. The Taft-Hartley Act represented an initiative that incorporated both the de-radicalization characteristic of McCarthy-era hysteria (anticommunist "loyalty oaths" were signed by some quarter-million trade union officials, while eleven unions were expelled from the CIO for refusing to sign) and the process of trade union bureaucratization (for example, leaders were required by the act to become disciplinarians over the rank and file, and union representation became a status that had to be officially certified in a government-controlled union election, rather than enforced by the collective strength of workers on the shop floor).

3. Most labor contracts disallow strikes during contractual periods, thus eliminating unexpected work stoppages. Grievance systems in American labor contracts normally channel worker complaints away from the shop floor and away from the workers themselves, to ever higher levels of managers and union officials.

4. Quoted in Zieger, "George Meany," p. 326.

5. Lichtenstein, *State of the Union*, ch. 3.

6. Fink, *Biographical Dictionary of American Labor Leaders*, p. 65.

7. Fink, *Biographical Dictionary of American Labor*, p. 10.

8. Data from ibid., pp. 8–9.

9. Some of the most prominent labor personalities on American television in the 1960s and 1970s were Jimmy Hoffa Sr., a tough-talking former leader of the Teamsters Union (the union of truck drivers), George Meany, a cigar-chewing and plain-speaking former plumber who headed the AFL-CIO from 1955 until his death in 1979, and Cesar Chavez, a charismatic leader who led a celebrated grape boycott as head of a union of mostly immigrant agricultural laborers. We expressly say "invisible man" because until very recently, and continuing in many labor organizations, the leadership of American trade unions has been almost exclusively a male fraternity.

10. Whyte's *The Organization Man* was a classic study of the postwar

business executive, whose singular drive to mount the corporate ladder produced a deep cultural and stylistic conformity.

11. After the war, Kirkland entered the School of Foreign Service at Georgetown University and after graduation worked as a research specialist on pensions and Social Security for the AF of L. In 1960, he was appointed executive assistant to George Meany, and in 1969 was selected by Meany to be secretary-treasurer of the AFL-CIO, the number-two position in the federation. Throughout his career Kirkland's most fervent interests were in international affairs, and he used his position at the AFL-CIO to keep American labor on an inflexible anticommunist course, showing complete support for all major U.S. government military and foreign policy initiatives (see Buhle, *Taking Care of Business*).

12. In 1881 an opposition candidate was elected in the largest local of Samuel Gompers's Cigar Makers International Union. Adolph Strasser, the "boss" of the union, responded to this challenge by nullifying the election and choosing a loyal follower to head the local union. Not long afterward, Terence Powderly, head of the rival Knights of Labor, also orchestrated the expulsion of several of his harshest critics. And in 1909, Dan Tobin of the Teamsters (a union notorious for nourishing corrupt "strongmen" at the top) wrote to a friend, "I am in hope that some day we will have peace but the next time we have peace it will be when those who are wrong will be cut out of the general membership" (see Van Time, *Making of a Labor Bureaucrat*, p. 111).

13. Quote of Jonathan Palewicz in the published obituary of Edward Hanley in the *New York Times*, January 16, 2000, p. 27.

14. Biers, "Hotel Employees President 'Retires' Under Pressure." In addition, a federal monitor found that Hanley had been receiving money, for no work, from a Chicago union local run by one of his sons, and that he had chartered a false union near his Wisconsin vacation home simply so that the local's "president" could do favors for Hanley and his friends.

15. Greenhouse, "Union Chief's Last Paycheck: $1.5 Million."

16. Greenhouse, "Ex-Union Chief's Palatial Penthouse."

17. "Sultanism" was Max Weber's term for the extreme form of pat-

rimonial domination that was exercised in early China and was characterized by personal absolutism and the subjectification of citizens. See Parsons, *Max Weber*, pp. 62, 347. Patrimonialism, as "a form of traditional political domination in which a royal household exercises arbitrary power through a bureaucratic apparatus," was a form that could be a fairly reasonable description of political practice in many American trade unions (see "Patrimonialism" in Abercrombie, Hill, and Turner, *Penguin Dictionary of Sociology*).

18. Benson, "Rising Tide of Union Democracy."

19. A history of one local plumbers and pipefitters' union indicates that on any given job a foreman might himself have been a journeyman plumber on another job two weeks previously, while one of the journeymen under his authority might very well become his foreman on a future job. Plus, good humor might prove as important as technical skill in successfully completing a job when two men are working very closely together for many weeks (see Scheirov, *Pride and Solidarity*, pp. 14–15).

20. The social logic of craft unionism is based on a weak pull toward social inclusion (a solidarity that tends to be limited to the brotherhood of the craft) combined with a much more forceful push of exclusionary practices that derive from the business unionist notion of the union as an enterprise that seeks the highest price for the labor power that it brokers. Because it is in the short-term interest of the skilled journeyman to limit the supply of labor, craft unionism is always predisposed toward exclusion. This is why craft unions throw up hurdles of various kinds to otherwise qualified journeymen seeking membership, like stringent skills tests and long apprenticeships, while often maintaining unofficial, but no less rigid social barriers along racial, ethnic, and gender lines. We would expect ideological variation within the craft union to be conditioned and therefore limited by this logic, which perhaps explains why one study of a craft union identified only two types of union members: the "steady Eddie," who tends to maintain close relations with the foreman; and the "union man," who tends to have a more solidaristic orientation and is more antagonistic to the foreman (see Schneirov, *Pride and Solidarity*).

21. Names like Hoffa (senior and junior) in the Teamsters Union, Hutcheson in the Carpenters Union, and Fosco or Coia in the Laborers Union are just a few of the "family dynasties" that have dominated in certain trade unions. There is an obvious irony in the fact that it is in relatively decentralized unions that local chieftains are able to garner the clout required to mount an effort to gain power at the national level, power that is then consolidated through acts of organizational centralization.

22. The small, but well-known United Electrical Workers (UE) is one such union that departs from most of the characteristics mentioned. For a good history of the UE, see Matles and Higgins, *Them and Us.* For a good overview of the history of the communists in American unions, see Cochran, *Labor and Communism.* The list of characteristics have been adapted and modified from Banks and Russo, "Teaching the Organizing Model of Unionism."

23. At the time this interview with Rogers was published, in 1989, the Carpenters Union had lost one-third of its membership in less than a decade (from 900,000 to 600,000 members between 1980 and 1989), a decline that was at least partly a result of the "union-busting" actions of employer groups such as the Associated Builders and Contractors.

24. Sweeney, now the president of the AFL-CIO, was head of the fast-growing Service Employees International Union (SEIU); Trumka, the vice president, was the leader of the United Mine Workers of America (UMWA), a union whose celebrated history gives it a symbolic weight out of all proportion to its relatively small membership; and the secretary-treasurer Linda Chavez-Thompson, former leader of the American Federation of State, County, and Municipal Employees (AFSCME), whose Latina ethnic heritage and gender personify two important social constituencies that have traditionally been underrepresented in the ranks of national union leadership.

25. The president of the federation is elected at a convention by delegates representing the affiliated trade unions, who cast numbers of votes in proportion to the size of their union membership.

26. Quaglieri, "People's Person," p. 99.

27. Juravich and Bronfenbrenner, "Preparing for the Worst."

28. Piore, "Unions," p. 527.

29. Ibid., p. 526.

30. Kilborn, "Bringing Down Labor's Giant Leader."

31. See Kilborn, "Bringing Down Labor's Giant Leader"; see also Dark, *Unions and the Democrats*, pp. 178–84.

32. See Benson, "Rising Tide of Union Democracy."

33. A symbolically significant example of the shifting ideological tenor was represented by the participation of top AFL-CIO officials, along with hundreds of Massachusetts trade unionists in a May Day march and rally in Boston, Massachusetts, on May 1, 2001. Although the United States is its actual birthplace (the first May Day demonstration was held in Chicago in 1886 in the struggle for the eight-hour workday), May Day has not been recognized by the official labor movement for well over fifty years, with the day typically observed by small leftist groups in a handful of cities (see Foner, *May Day*). Traditionally, the American "Labor Day" is held in early September and since the early twentieth century has been a completely apolitical holiday, a day off from work that signals the final weekend of summer, and a day when American families gather for outdoor barbecues. Consequently, not only is it remarkable that trade unionists were mobilized by their leaders to attend a march and rally on May Day, but that AFL-CIO President John Sweeney addressed the rally, reportedly making a forceful speech advancing the rights of immigrants and declaring union solidarity with immigrant workers.

34. In their systematic analysis of recent union organizing, Bronfenbrenner and Hickey identify these unions as having achieved major organizing victories and as being key players in the contemporary labor movement. Even among this small group, however, SEIU, HERE, and UNITE stand out as being the most innovative and comprehensive in their organizing (see Bronfenbrenner and Hickey, "Changing to Organize").

35. Many of these same points have been made in Fantasia, "Myth of the Labor Movement," and have been illustrated empirically in Fantasia, *Cultures of Solidarity*.

36. See Form, *Segmented Labor, Fractured Politics*, a careful study of labor's political efforts in one state (Ohio), which offers ample justification for the author's depressingly pessimistic account of labor politics in the United States. Its only hopeful aspect is that it was written prior to the rise of the New Voice leadership.

37. See Dean, "Road to Union City," especially pp. 164–65. In Western Massachusetts, home of one of the authors, the local central labor council has been quite thoroughly transformed in recent years. What was once an insular organization with a minimal public presence (and which completely shunned radical social activism of any kind), the current labor council is a designated "Union Cities" project that is led by militant unionists who are willing to work alongside radicals and activist community groups and who routinely mount protest actions against local employers on behalf of aggrieved workers. Although still small in scale, the labor movement in western Massachusetts has a more prominent public face, one with the character of a social movement.

38. Ness and Eimer, *Central Labor Councils*.

39. Early and Cohen, "Jobs with Justice"; Early and Wilson, "Health Care Reform."

40. For an overview of the conditions of labor of garment workers in the United States, see Ross, *No Sweat*; and Bonacich and Appelbaum, *Behind the Label*.

41. J. Gordon, "Immigrants Fight the Power"; Ness, "Organizing Immigrant Communities."

42. Greenhouse, "In U.S. Unions, Mexico Finds Unlikely Ally on Immigration."

43. Data examined for this project show that the median age of the thirty-four members 1976 AFL-CIO Executive Council was 62 years old. As Table 3.1 indicates, the average age of the union leadership was 53.7 years in 1976, and this would have included local, regional, and national leaders (the average age of national leaders alone was 56.8 years in 1976). Thirteen of the thirty-four members of the 1976 executive council attended university, while twenty-nine of the current fifty-two council members have attended university. But if we consider the leaders of

national unions overall for 1976, the percent that attended university is significantly higher (52 percent) than on the executive council and closer to the level of educational attainment for the members of the current council (56 percent). For data on the 1976 overall national union leadership, see Fink, *Biographical Dictionary of American Labor Leaders*, p. 71.

44. Several members of this cohort, such as Andy Stern, John Wilhelm, and Bruce Raynor, are heads of unions and thus have been elected by union members. But, with the partial exception of those in HERE, most of the new militants do not have an independent membership base and therefore are vulnerable to political winds and pressures. For example, Richard Bensinger, who was appointed director of organizing by Sweeney and was charged with overseeing a massive increase in the federation's organizing activities, was reportedly forced to resign his post by Sweeney after angering conservative members of the federation's executive council with his aggressive and militant leadership style.

45. See Voss and Sherman, "Breaking the Iron Law of Oligarchy," for an elaboration on what some of these experiences were and how they were applied in innovative union-organizing campaigns.

46. See Lerner, "Organizing Strategies for the 21st Century."

47. Some of the labor leaders who participated in these conferences, in addition to the triumvirate of Sweeney, Trumka, and Chavez-Thompson, were Ron Blackwell, the head of corporate affairs, Bill Fletcher Jr., former education director, and Karen Nussbaum, previous head of what was once the federation's Working Women Department. Their speeches appear, along with others who participated in these gatherings, in Fraser and Freeman, *Audacious Democracy*. See also Alterman, "Intellectuals and Workers Close Ranks."

48. Some examples are: the Sociology Labor Network, which has since metamorphosed into the Labor and Labor Movements' Section of the American Sociological Association; Scholars, Artists, and Writers for Social Justice, an organization that has since disbanded; and the ongoing journal, *New Labor Forum*, which provides a place for academics, labor activists, and community organizers to "test new ideas and debate old ones." Two years after the teach-ins, several labor historians

created a new group, the Labor and Working-Class History Association, dedicated in part to forging a new alliance between intellectuals and union activists. Less formal networks were also forged, some of which have been ongoing, like the Organizing Research Network (ORN), coordinated by the Economic Policy Institute.

CHAPTER 4: PRACTICES AND POSSIBILITIES OF A SOCIAL MOVEMENT UNIONISM

1. In 1999, UNITE organized the largest textile plant in America, which had stood for ninety-three years as a symbol of resistance to unionization in the American South. When in July 2003, the company announced it was going out of business, people began to highlight this bankruptcy as a prime example of why unionization is risky. However, such reasoning is wrong, as two economists, John DiNardo and David Lee, have demonstrated. Their rigorous quantitative analysis of more than 27,000 union-certification elections between 1983 and 2000 shows that successfully unionized establishments are no less likely to survive in the marketplace than their nonunion counterparts. In the case of the textile industry, one need only consider that *most* textile plants in the South have *never* been unionized — yet almost all of them have gone out of business or moved to low-wage countries — to see that unionization is not the reason for the collapse of the textile industry in the United States. See DiNardo and Lee, "Unionism in California and the U.S."

2. Western, *Between Class and Market.*

3. As we reported in Chapter 2, between 1985 and 1989 permanent-replacement workers were hired in one-third of all strikes, and the threat of replacement workers was used in many others. See Schnell and Gramm, "Empirical Relations."

4. Between 1989 and 1994, for example, three out of five organizing drives were lost in the manufacturing sector, where unions had once been especially successful, winning the overwhelming majority of their campaigns. See the Bureau of National Affairs, "NLRB Representation and Decertification Elections Statistics," May 1994 for statistics on 1989.

When unions won organizing drives, employers had yet another weapon in their arsenal of antilabor practices: they stalled negotiations for the first labor agreement until workers lost faith in the union. For examples of these practices, see Human Rights Watch, *Unfair Advantage*.

5. Statistics for these statements are provided above in Chapter 2.

6. Cobble, "Making Postindustrial Unionism Possible," p. 302.

7. For statistical evidence showing that institutions mediate the effect of structural economic changes in explaining union decline, see Western, *Between Class and Market*, pp. 150–55. See also Mishel, Bernstein, and Schmitt, *State of Working America 2000 2001*, pp. 168–72.

8. Figure from Bronfenbrenner et al., "Introduction," p. 5.

9. *U.S. News and World Report*, February 21, 1972, quoted in Nissen, *Which Direction for Organized Labor?* p. 15.

10. Quotes and examples are taken from Voss and Sherman, "Breaking the Iron Law of Oligarchy."

11. R. L. Freeman, "What Does the Future Hold for U.S. Unionism?"

12. Lerner, "Reviving Unions."

13. At least one right-wing academic, Jarol B. Manheim, tries to use this history to delegitimize the corporate campaign (see his *Death by a Thousand Cuts*), but labor intellectuals also readily acknowledge the link. See, for example, the quote of the labor lawyer in Voss and Sherman, *Breaking the Iron Law of Oligarchy*, pp. 330–31.

14. Lopez, *Reorganizing the Rust Belt*.

15. In 1996, *Newsweek* published an article entitled, "It's Hip to be Union." Following the success of Union Summer, the AFL-CIO launched Senior Summer, for retired Americans, and Seminary Summer, for religious leaders.

16. This had been the experience in SEIU, where Sweeney had pushed a similar program. Locals that had once spent only 2 or 3 percent of their budgets on recruitment discovered that upping that amount to 30 percent fundamentally altered their day-to-day work. No longer able to afford so many business agents, locals began to train rank-and-file members to deal with troubles on the job. They also began to hire and

train more organizers, who tended to be female and minority, like the workers they were trying to unionize. Locals also launched programs to teach members how to help with organizing drives. Together, these organizational changes altered union culture, promoting new levels of participation and commitment. Sweeney sought a similar change throughout the AFL-CIO. See Voss and Sherman, *Breaking the Iron Law of Oligarchy;* and Fletcher and Hurd, "Political Will, Local Union Transformation."

17. The number "six" is based on our own reading of the evidence, and on Bronfenbrenner and Hickey's analysis of unions using comprehensive organizing tactics and winning major organizing victories. See their article, "Changing to Organize." The six include SEIU, HERE, UNITE, CWA, AFSCME, and the higher-education division of the UAW. (Even among this small group, SEIU, HERE, and UNITE stand out for running campaigns that use the most tactics in the repertoire of social movement unionism.) Others put the number of "organizing unions" higher, usually at ten, but include unions that do not use social movement practices in their campaigns. Figures on the percentage of AFL-CIO membership in each of these unions is taken from Lerner, "Immodest Proposal," p. 15.

18. Carl Somers provided very helpful research assistance for this section and the Las Vegas section.

19. Howley, "Justice for Janitors."

20. On the relationship between trusteeship and union transformation, see Voss and Sherman, *Breaking the Iron Law of Oligarchy;* and Lerner, "Organizing Strategies for the 21st Century."

21. See Howley, "Justice for Janitors"; Lerner, "Reviving Unions."

22. This phrase appeared over every *Los Angeles Times* editorial until the early 1960s. See Davis, *City of Quartz.*

23. Quoted in Waldinger et al., "Helots No More," p. 19.

24. Milkman, "Immigrant Organizing."

25. Waldinger et al., "Helots No More," pp. 106–8; Nazario, "For This Union, It's War."

26. Fisk, Mitchell, and Erickson, "Union Representation of Immigrant Janitors in Southern California," pp. 203, 207–11.

27. Milkman and Wong, "Organizing Immigrant Workers," pp. 108–9; Lerner, "Reviving Unions."

28. Lerner, "Reviving Unions."

29. Quoted in Waldinger et al., "Helots No More," p. 114.

30. Nazario, "For This Union, It's War"; Waldinger et al., "Helots No More"; and Torres, "Talking Trash."

31. Erickson et al., "Justice for Janitors in Los Angles and Beyond," is an especially good source for political alliances and pressure points in both the first J for J campaign and the 2000 contract negotiations.

32. Brecher, *Strike!* p. 343.

33. Torres, "Talking Trash"; Baker, "Police Use Force to Block Strike March."

34. See Erickson et al., "Justice for Janitors in Los Angeles and Beyond," who also report that Bevona was later forced out of office by opponents who wanted their local to use J for J tactics in New York City.

35. Waldinger et al., "Helots No More"; figure from Silverman and Meyer, "Fast Growing Union Hits Obstacles in L.A."

36. Milkman, "Immigrant Organizing." For additional examples of the militancy some immigrants bring from their home countries, see Pimentel, "Immigrant Organizers Strengthen U.S. Unions."

37. Greenhouse, "Biggest Drive Since 1937."

38. Meyerson, "Clean Sweep."

39. On the internal struggles in Local 399, see Nazario, "Hunger Strike Marks Union's Split"; Silverman and Meyer, "Fast Growing Union Hits Obstacles in L.A."; and Bacon, "Western Janitors." On the correlation between social movement unionism and internal organizational transformation, see Voss and Sherman, *Breaking the Iron Law of Oligarchy*.

40. Meyerson, "Street vs. Suite."

41. See Meyerson, "Clean Sweep"; and Erickson et al., "Justice for Janitors in Los Angeles and Beyond."

42. See Cleeland and Rabin, "Gore's Presence at Rally Boosts Janitor's Spirits"; Cleeland, "L.A. Janitors OK Contract in Landmark Vote"; Meyerson, "Street vs. Suite"; and Erickson et al., "Justice for Janitors in Los Angeles and Beyond."

43. Bacon, "L.A. Transit Strike Forges New Political Alliances"; Trevino, "Strike Allies." See also Davis, *Magical Urbanism*, pp. 167–75.

44. See Moehring, *Resort City in the Sunbelt;* and Daly, "Dynasty of Rogues," p. 40.

45. Davis, "Class Struggle in Oz"; Cannon, "Las Vegas's Service Industry Workers."

46. Davis, "Class Struggle in Oz"; Alexander, "Rise to Power."

47. Hurd, "Bottom-Up Organizing"; Serrin, "Unorthodox Heads Unionists at Yale."

48. On the high level of worker solidarity, see Serrin, "Labor Pact at Yale." In interviews Rachel Sherman and Kim Voss did with HERE activists in California in the late 1990s, many identified the Yale campaign as having provided a model for how to build rank-and-file committees (see Sherman and Voss, "Organize or Die").

49. See, for example, the AFL-CIO magazine, *America @Work*, June 2001.

50. The strike was covered in both the local and national press. Especially helpful accounts can be found in Cannon, "Las Vegas's Service Industry"; Davis, "Class Struggle in Oz"; Baker, "Union Workers' March Is an Uphill Battle"; Ferrell, "179 Arrested In Sit-in Outside Las Vegas"; Bach, "AFL-CIO to Tackle Long-running Strike"; Bacon, "Frontier Casino Workers Outlast Union Busters"; and Mosle, "At Hotel Casino, Triumphant Shouts of 'Union!'"

51. See, for example, Binkley, "At Some Casinos, the Worst Enemy Isn't a Card Counter."

52. Cannon, "Las Vegas's Service Industry Workers"; Greenhouse, "Labor Rolls on in Las Vegas"; D. Lewis, "Labor Movement's Jackpot."

53. Moberg, "Organization Man"; Greenhouse, "Labor Rolls on in Las Vegas."

54. The quote is from Greenhouse, "Labor Rolls on in Las Vegas." Accounts of Local 226's internal organization can be found in Moberg, "Organization Man," pp. 23–29; and Davis, "Class Struggle in Oz."

55. For example, the housekeeping staffs at unionized Las Vegas hotels are paid almost double what maids earn at nonunion hotels in

other cities. Las Vegas is now the only American city where low-end service workers are paid enough to own their own homes.

56. Moberg, "Unions Get Religion"; Gerrie, "Unions."

57. Figures are from Hirsch and Macpherson, "Union Membership and Coverage Database," who report that the private-sector unionization rate in Las Vegas is 14.8, and in the United States 8.6.

CHAPTER 5: TWO FUTURES

1. Fantasia and Voss, "Bush Administration's Low-Intensity War Against Labor."

2. Bacon, "Dockworkers' Contract Postpones Crucial Jurisdiction Questions," p. 1.

3. See Chapter 4, above. Together, these six unions represent about one-third of the total membership of the AFL-CIO.

4. Moberg, "Union Cities"; see also Kriesky, "Structural Change in the AFL-CIO."

5. See McAlevey, "It Takes a Community"; and Clawson, *Next Upsurge*.

6. See Pollin and Luce, *Living Wage*; Economic Policy Institute, *Living Wage: Facts at a Glance*.

7. Gourevitch, "Awakening the Giant."

8. Van Voorhis, "Hub Janitors Reach Deal, End Strike"; Barlow, "Faith Takes a Seat at Bargaining Table."

9. Greenhouse, "Activism Surges at Campuses Nationwide."

WORKS CITED

Abercrombie, Nicholas, Stephen Hill, and Bryan S. Turner. *The Penguin Dictionary of Sociology*. New York: Viking Penguin, 1988.

Abraham, Katharine, and Susan Houseman. "Job Security in America: A Better Approach." *Brookings Review* 11 (1993): 34–36.

Ackerman, Seth. "Supply-Side Journalism." *Harper's Magazine*, October 1999, pp. 66–67.

Alexander, Courtney. "Rise to Power: The Recent History of the Culinary Union in Las Vegas." In *The Grit Beneath the Glitter: Tales from the Real Las Vegas*, ed. Hal K. Rothman and Mike Davis, pp. 145–75. Berkeley and Los Angeles: University of California Press, 2002.

Alterman, Eric. "Intellectuals and Workers Close Ranks." *Le Monde Diplomatique*, December 1997, p. 12.

Amenta, Edwin, and Theda Skocpol. "Redefining the New Deal: World War II and the Development of Social Provision in the United States." In *The Politics of Social Policy in the United States*, ed. Margaret Weir, Ann Shola Orloff, and Theda Skocpol, pp. 81–122. Princeton, N.J.: Princeton University Press, 1988.

Anderson, Sarah, John Cavanagh, Chris Harman, and Betsy Loendar-Wright. *Executive Excess 2001*. Institute for Policy Studies and United for a Fair Economy, 2001.

Archer, Robin. "Does Repression Help Create Labor Parties? The Effects of Police and Military Intervention on Unions in the United States and Australia." *Studies in American Political Development* 15 (2001): 189–219.

Bach, Lisa Kim. "AFL-CIO to Tackle Long-Running Strike." *Las Vegas Review Journal*, February 20, 1997, p. D1.

Bacon, David. "Dockworkers' Contract Postpones Crucial Jurisdiction Questions." *Labor Notes*, February 2003, p. 1.

———. "Frontier Casino Workers Outlast Union Busters." *In These Times*, January 11, 1998, p. 7.

———. "Immigrants Find High-Tech Servitude in Silicon Valley." *Labor Notes*, September 2000, pp. 3–4.

———. "L.A. Transit Strike Forges New Political Alliances." *Jinn Magazine* online, October 20, 2000. http://www.pacificnews.org/jinn/stories/6.21/001020-la.html

———. "Western Janitors . . . Keep Your Eyes on Spring." *Jinn Magazine* online, March 7, 1997. http://www.pacificnews.org/jinn/toc/3.07.html

Baker, Bob. "Police Use Force to Block Strike March." *Los Angeles Times*, June 16, 1990, p. B1.

———. "Union Workers' March Is an Uphill Battle." *Los Angeles Times*, January 7, 1992, p. A3.

Banks, Anthony, and John Russo. "Teaching the Organizing Model of Unionism and Campaign-Based Education." Unpublished manuscript presented at the AFL-CIO/Cornell University Research Conference on Union Organizing, Washington, D.C., 1996.

Barlow, Rich. "Faith Takes a Seat at Bargaining Table." *The Boston Globe*, October 12, 2002, p. B2.

Bell, Daniel. "The Capitalism of the Proletariat: A Theory of American Trade Unionism." In *The End of Ideology*, pp. 211–26. Cambridge, Mass.: Harvard University Press, 1960.

———. *The End of Ideology*. Glencoe, Ill.: The Free Press, 1960.

Benson, Herman. "A Rising Tide of Union Democracy." In *The Trans-*

formation of U.S. Unions, ed. Ray M. Tillman and Michael S. Cummings, pp. 27–47. Boulder, Colo.: Lynne Rienner Publishers, 1999.

Bergmann, Barbara R. *Saving Our Children from Poverty: What the United States Can Learn from France*. New York: Russell Sage Foundation, 1996.

Biers, Carl. "Hotel Employees President 'Retires' Under Pressure." *Labor Notes*, July 1998, p. 1.

Binkley, Christina. "At Some Casinos, the Worst Enemy Isn't a Card Counter." *Wall Street Journal*, June 7, 1999, p. A1.

Blank, Rebecca. "Does a Larger Social Safety Net Mean Less Economic Flexibility?" In *Working Under Different Rules*, ed. Richard B. Freeman, pp. 157–87. New York: Russell Sage Foundation, 1994.

Blau, Francine D., and Lawrence M. Kahn. "International Differences in Male Wage Inequality: Institutions Versus Market Forces." *Journal of Political Economy* 104 (1966): 791–837.

Bonacich, Edna, and Richard P. Appelbaum. *Behind the Label: Inequality in the Los Angeles Apparel Industry*. Berkeley and Los Angeles: University of California Press, 2000.

Bourdieu, Pierre. "Social Space and the Genesis of 'Classes.'" In *Language and Symbolic Power*, pp. 229–51. Cambridge, Mass.: Harvard University Press, 1991.

Boyer, Richard O., and Herbert M. Morais. *Labor's Untold Story*. New York: United Electrical, Radio, and Machine Workers of America, 1955.

Brecher, Jeremy. *Strike!* Revised and updated edition. Boston: South End Press, 1997.

Brody, David. "Labor Elections: Good for Workers?" *Dissent* (summer 1997): 71–77.

———. *Workers in Industrial America*. New York: Oxford University Press, 1980.

Bronfenbrenner, Kate, Sheldon Friedman, Richard W. Hurd, Rudolph A. Oswald and Ronald L. Seebe. "Introduction." In *Organizing to Win: New Research on Union Strategies*, pp. 1–15. Ithaca, N.Y.: Cornell University Press, 1998.

Bronfenbrenner, Kate, and Robert Hickey. "Changing to Organize: A National Assessment of Union Strategies," In *Rebuilding Labor: Organizing and Organizers in the New Labor Movement*, ed. Ruth Milkman and Kim Voss. Ithaca, N.Y.: Cornell University Press, forthcoming.

Buhle, Paul. "Samuel Gompers and Business Unionism." In *Taking Care of Business: Samuel Gompers, George Meany, Lane Kirkland, and the Tragedy of American Labor*. New York: Monthly Review Press, 1999.

———. *Taking Care of Business: Samuel Gompers, George Meany, Lane Kirkland, and the Tragedy of American Labor*. New York: Monthly Review Press, 1999.

Cannon, Lou. "Las Vegas's Service Industry Workers Hit the Jackpot with Union Contracts." *The Washington Post*, November 30, 1997, p. A3.

Chamberlain, Neil W. *The Union Challenge to Management Control*. New York: Harper Collins, 1948.

Clawson, Dan. *The Next Upsurge: Labor and the New Social Movements*. Ithaca, N.Y.: Cornell University Press, 2003.

Cleeland , Nancy. "L.A. Strikers OK Contract in Landmark Vote." *Los Angeles Times*, April 25, 2000. http://latimes.com/news/state20000425/t000038825.html

Cleeland , Nancy, and Jeffrey L. Rabin. "Gore's Presence at Rally Boosts Janitor's Spirits." *Los Angeles Times*, April 17, 2000. http://latimes.com/news/politics/elect2000/pres/money/20000417/t000036238.html

Cobble, Dorothy Sue. "Making Postindustrial Unionism Possible." In *Restoring the Promise of American Labor Law*, ed. Sheldon Friedman, Richard W. Hurd, Rudolph A. Oswald, and Ronald L. Seeber, pp. 285–302. Ithaca, N.Y.: ILR Press, 1994.

Cochran, Bert. *Labor and Communism: The Conflict that Shaped American Unions*. Princeton, N.J.: Princeton University Press, 1977.

Cohen, Lizabeth. *Making a New Deal: Industrial Workers in Chicago, 1919–1939*. New York: Cambridge University Press, 1990.

Cumbler, John. *Working Class Community in Industrial America*. Westport, Conn.: Greenwood Publishers, 1979.

Daly, John. "A Dynasty of Rogues: The Teamsters' History of Corruption." *Maclean's*, March 23, 1992, pp. 36–42.

Dark, Taylor E. *The Unions and the Democrats: An Enduring Alliance.* Ithaca, N.Y.: Cornell University Press, 1999.

Davis, Mike. *City of Quartz.* New York: Verso, 1991.

———. "Class Struggle in Oz." In *The Grit Beneath the Glitter: Tales from the Real Las Vegas,* ed. Hal K. Rothman and Mike Davis, pp. 176–84. Berkeley and Los Angeles: University of California Press, 2002.

———. *Magical Urbanism: Latinos Reinvent the U.S. City.* New York: Verso, 2001.

Dean, Amy B. "The Road to Union City: Building the Labor Movement Citywide." In *Not Your Father's Union Movement,* ed. Jo-Ann Mort. New York: Verso, 1998.

Early, Steve, and Larry Cohen. "Jobs with Justice. Building a Broad Based Movement for Workers' Rights." *Social Policy* (1994): 7–18.

Early, Steve, and Rand Wilson. "Health Care Reform from the Bottom Up." *New Politics* (1992): 109–14.

Economic Policy Institute. *Living Wage: Facts at a Glance.* http://www.epinet.org/content.cfm/issueguides_livingwage_livingwagefacts

Ehrenreich, Barbara. *Nickel and Dimed: On (Not) Getting By in America.* New York: Henry Holt and Co., 2001.

Enrich, David. "High-Tech Cheap Labor." *The Nation,* October 16, 2000, p. 7.

Erickson, Christopher L., Catharine Fisk, Ruth Milkman, Daniel J. B. Mitchell, and Kent Wong. "Justice for Janitors in Los Angeles and Beyond: A New Form of Unionism in the 21st Century and Beyond?" In *Changing Role of Unions: New Forms of Representation,* ed. Phanindra V. Wunnava. Armonk, N.Y.: M. E. Sharpe, forthcoming.

Ernsberger, Richard Jr. "Wal-Mart World." *Newsweek,* May 20, 2002, p. 50.

Fantasia, Rick. "The Assault on American Labor." In *Social Problems,* ed. Craig Calhoun and George Ritzer, pp. 663–79. New York: McGraw-Hill Inc., 1993.

———. *Cultures of Solidarity: Consciousness, Action, and Contemporary*

American Workers. Berkeley and Los Angeles: University of California Press, 1988.

———. "Dictature sur le proletariat." *ACTES de la recherché en science sociales* 138 (2001): 3–18.

———. "The Myth of the Labor Movement." In *The Blackwell Companion to Sociology*, ed. Judith R. Blau, pp. 450–63. Malden, Mass.: Blackwell Publishers, 2001.

Fantasia, Rick, and Judith Stepan-Norris. "Labor in Action." In *The Blackwell Companion to Social Movements*, ed. D. Snow, S. Soule, and H. Kriesi. Malden, Mass.: Blackwell Publishers, forthcoming.

Fantasia, Rick, and Kim Voss. "Bush Administration's Low-Intensity War Against Labor." *Le Monde Diplomatique*, June 2003, p. 14.

Ferrell, David. "179 Arrested in Sit-in Outside Las Vegas Hotel." *Los Angeles Times*, September 8, 1992, p. A26.

Fink, Gary M. *Biographical Dictionary of American Labor.* Westport, Conn.: Greenwood Press, 1984.

———. *Biographical Dictionary of American Labor Leaders.* Westport, Conn.: Greenwood Press, 1974.

Fischer, Claude, Michael Hout, Martin Sanchez Jankowski, Samuel R. Lucas, Ann Swidler, and Kim Voss. *Inequality by Design.* Princeton, N.J.: Princeton University Press, 1996.

———. "Myths about Inequality in America." Survey Research Center Working Paper, Berkeley, California, July 1996.

Fisk, Catherine L., Daniel J. B. Mitchell, and Christopher L. Erickson, "Union Representation of Immigrant Janitors in Southern California: Economic and Legal Challenges." In *Organizing Immigrants: The Challenge for Unions in Contemporary California*, ed. Ruth Milkman, pp. 199–224. Berkeley and Los Angeles: University of California Press, 2000.

Fletcher, Bill Jr., and Richard W. Hurd. "Political Will, Local Union Transformation, and the Organizing Imperative." In *Which Direction for Organized Labor? Essays on Organizing, Outreach, and Internal Transformations*, ed. Bruce Nissen, pp. 191–216. Detroit, Mich.: Wayne State University Press, 1999.

Foner, Philip S. *May Day: A Short History of the International Workers' Holiday 1886–1986.* New York: Monthly Review Press, 1986.

"For Greenspan, Ease in Firing Is a U.S. Plus." *International Herald Tribune,* July 12, 2000, p. 3.

Form, William. *Segmented Labor, Fractured Politics.* New York: Plenum, 1995.

Fox, Alan. *History and Heritage: The Social Origins of the British Industrial Relations System.* London: Allen and Unwin, 1985.

Fraser, Steven, and Joshua B. Freeman, eds. *Audacious Democracy: Labor, Intellectuals, and the Social Reconstruction of America.* New York: Houghton Mifflin Co., 1997.

Freeman, Richard B. "How Labor Fares in Advanced Economies." In *Working Under Different Rules,* ed. Richard B. Freeman, pp. 19–28. New York: Russell Sage Foundation, 1994.

Freeman, Richard B., and Lawrence F. Katz, eds. *Differences and Changes in Wage Structures.* Chicago: University of Chicago Press, 1995.

Freeman, Richard R. "What Does the Future Hold for U.S. Unionism?" *Relations Industrielles* 441 (1989): 25–43.

Frey, William H., Bill Abresch, and Jonathan Yeasting. *America by the Numbers: A Field Guide to the U.S. Population.* New York: New Press, 2001.

Friedman, Gerald. "The State and the Making of the Working Class: France and the United States, 1880–1914." *Theory and Society* 17 (1988): 403–30.

Georgine, Robert. "From Brass Knuckles to Briefcases: The Modern Art of Union-Busting." In *The Big Business Reader,* ed. Mark Green and Robert Massie, pp. 89–104. New York: Pilgrim Press, 1980.

Gerber, Larry G. "Shifting Perspectives on American Exceptionalism: Recent Literature on American Labor Relations and Labor Politics." *Journal of American Studies* 31 (1997): 253–74.

Gerrie, Sharon. "Unions: Book Cites Labor Law Violations." *Las Vegas Review Journal,* June 13, 2001, p. D2.

Glaberman, Martin. *Wartime Strikes: The Struggle Against the No-Strike*

Pledge in the UAW During World War II. Detroit, Mich.: Bewick Editions, 1980.

Gordon, David, Richard Edwards, and Michael Reich. *Segmented Work, Divided Workers*. Cambridge: Cambridge University Press, 1982.

Gordon, Jennifer. "Immigrants Fight the Power." *The Nation*, January 3, 2000, pp. 16–20.

Granovetter, Mark. *Getting a Job*. Chicago: University of Chicago Press, 1995.

Gray, John. *False Dawn: The Delusions of Global Capitalism*. New York: New Press, 1998.

Green, James R. *The World of the Worker*. New York: Hill and Wang, 1980.

Greenhouse, Steven. "Activism Surges at Campuses Nationwide and Labor Is at Issue." *The New York Times*, March 29, 1999, p. A14.

———. "Amazon.com Is Using the Web to Block Unions' Efforts to Organize." *The New York Times*, November 29, 2000, p. C1.

———. "In Biggest Drive Since 1937, Union Gains a Victory." *The New York Times* February 26, 1999, p. A1.

———. "Ex-Union Chief's Palatial Penthouse." *The New York Times*, February 9, 1999, p. A23.

———. "Janitors Struggle at the Edges of Silicon Valley's Success." *The New York Times*, April 18, 2000, p. A12.

———. "Labor Leader Sounds Do-or-Die Warning." *The New York Times*, February 19, 2001, p. A10.

———. "Labor Rolls on in Las Vegas." *The New York Times*, April 27, 1998, p. A10.

———. "Suits Say Wal-Mart Forces Workers to Toil off the Clock." *The New York Times*, June 25, 2002, p. A1.

———. "Temp Workers at Microsoft Win Lawsuit." *The New York Times*, December 13, 2000, p. C1.

———. "Trying to Overcome Embarrassment, Labor Launches Drive to Organize Wal-Mart." *The New York Times*, November 8, 2002, p. A28.

————. "Union Chief's Last Paycheck: $1.5 Million." *The New York Times*, February 3, 1999, p. A17.

————. "Unions Need Not Apply." *The New York Times*, July 26, 1999, p. C1.

————. "Unions Pushing to Organize Thousands of Amazon.com Workers." *The New York Times*, November 23, 2000, p. C1.

————. "In U.S. Unions, Mexico Finds Unlikely Ally on Immigration." *The New York Times*, July 19, 2001, p. A1.

Gourevitch, Alexander. "Awakening the Giant: How the Living Wage Movement Can Revive Progressive Politics." *The American Prospect* online, May 30, 2001. http://www.prospect.org/webfeatures/2001/05/gourevitch-a-05-30.htmlv

Griffith, Robert, and Alan Theoharis, eds. *The Specter: Original Essays on the Cold War and the Origins of McCarthyism.* New York: New Viewpoints, 1974.

Harrington, Michael. *The Other America.* New York: Macmillan, 1962.

Helburn, Suzannne W., and Barbara R. Bergmann. *America's Childcare Problem: The Way Out.* New York: Palgrave/St. Martin's, 2000.

Hirsch, Barry T., and David A. Macpherson. "Union Membership and Coverage Database from the Current Population Survey: Note." *Industrial and Labor Relations Review* 56 (January 2003): 349–54. http://www.unionstats.com

Holt, James. "Trade Unionism in the British and U.S. Steel Industries, 1880 1914: A Comparative Study" In *The Labor History Reader*, ed. Daniel Leab, pp. 166–96. Urbana: University of Illinois Press, 1997.

Howley, John. "Justice for Janitors: The Challenge of Organizing in Contract Services." *Labor Research Review* 15 (1990): 61–71.

Human Rights Watch. *Unfair Advantage: Worker's Freedom of Association in the United States.* New York: Human Rights Watch, 2000.

Hurd, Richard W. "Bottom-Up Organizing: HERE in New Haven and Boston." *Labor Research Review* 5 (1986): 5–19.

————. "A Retrospective on the PATCO Strategy." In *The Air Controllers' Controversy: Lessons from the PATCO Strike*, ed. Arthur B.

Shostak and David Skocik, pp. 206–14. New York: Human Sciences Press, Inc., 1986.

Jackson, Justin. "Newswatch." *Labor Notes*, November 2000, p. 4.

Jacoby, Sanford. "American Exceptionalism Revisited: The Importance of Management." In *Masters to Managers: Historical and Comparative Perspectives on American Employers*, pp. 173–200. New York: Columbia University Press, 1991.

———, ed. *Masters to Managers: Historical and Comparative Perspectives on American Employers*. New York: Columbia University Press, 1991.

———. *Modern Manors: Welfare Capitalism Since the New Deal*. Princeton, N.J.: Princeton University Press, 1997.

Juravich, Tom, and Kate Bronfenbrenner. "Preparing for the Worst: Organizing and Staying Organized in the Public Sector." In *Organizing to Win: New Research on Union Strategies*, ed. Kate Bronfenbrenner, Sheldon Friedman, Richard W. Hurd, Rudolph A. Oswald, and Ronald L. Seeber, pp. 261–82. Ithaca, N.Y.: Cornell University Press, 1998.

———. *Ravenswood: The Steelworkers' Victory and the Revival of American Labor*. Ithaca, N.Y.: Cornell University Press, 1999.

Karabel, Jerome. "The Failure of American Socialism Reconsidered." In *The Socialist Register*, ed. Ralph Miliband and John Saville, pp. 204–27. London: Merlin Press, 1979.

Kassarda, John D. "Industrial Restructuring and the Changing Location of Jobs." In *State of the Union: America in the 1990s*, vol. 1, ed. Reynolds Farley, pp. 215–68. New York: Russell Sage Foundation, 1995.

Kaufman, Leslie. "As Biggest Business, Wal-Mart Propels Changes Elsewhere." *The New York Times*, October 22, 2000, p. A1.

Kilborn, Peter T. "Bringing Down Labor's Giant Leader." *The New York Times*, September 4, 1995, p. A7.

Kingsolver, Barbara. *Holding the Line: Women in the Great Arizona Mine Strike of 1983*. Ithaca, N.Y.: ILR Press, 1989.

Klein, Naomi. *No Logo: Taking Aim at the Brand Bullies*. New York: Picador, 1999.

Klinger, Scott, Chris Harman, Sarah Anderson, John Cavanagh, and

Holly Sklar, *Executive Excess*. Washington, D.C: Institute for Policy Studies, 2002.

Kochan, Thomas A., Harry C. Katz, and Robert B. McKersie. *The Transformation of American Industrial Relations*. Ithaca, N.Y.: Cornell University Press, 1994.

Kriesky, Jill. "Structural Change in the AFL-CIO: A Regional Study of Union Cities' Impact." In *Rekindling the Movement: Labor's Quest for Relevance in the Twenty-First Century*, ed. Lowell Turner, Harry C. Katz, and Richard W. Hurd, pp. 129–54. Ithaca, N.Y.: Cornell University Press, 2001.

Krugman, Paul. "For Richer: How the Permissive Capitalism of the Boom Destroyed American Equality." *The New York Times Magazine*, October 20, 2002, pp. 66–67.

Lang, Anne Adams. "Behind the Prosperity, Working People in Trouble." *The New York Times*, November 20, 2000, p. F21.

Lavelle, Louis, "Executive Compensation Survey," *Business Week*, April 15, 2002.

Leibovich, Mark. "Service Without a Smile." *The Washington Post National Weekly Edition*, December 13, 1999, pp. 9–10.

Lerner, Steven. "An Immodest Proposal: A New Architecture for the House of Labor." *New Labor Forum* 12, no. 2 (summer 2003): 9–30.

———. "Organizing Strategies for the 21st Century." Presentation to the Conference on "The New Economy and Union Responses," University of California, Institute for Labor and Employment, Los Angeles, March 9, 2001. Summary of Proceedings: http://ucop.edu/ile/conferences/march_conf/index.html

———. "Reviving Unions." *Boston Review* online 21 (1996). http://bostonreview.mit.edu/BR21.2/lerner.html

Levinson, Marc. "It's Hip to be Union." *Newsweek*, July 8, 1996, p. 44.

Lewis, Diane E. "The Labor Movement's Jackpot." *The Boston Globe*, October 6, 1999, p. A1.

Lewis, Michael. "In Defense of the Boom." *The New York Times*, October 27, 2002, 44–49, 60, 70–71, 84.

Lichtenstein, Nelson. *Labor's War at Home*. Cambridge: Cambridge University Press, 1982.

———. *State of the Union: A Century of America Labor*. Princeton, N.J.: Princeton University Press, 2002.

———. *Walter Reuther: The Most Dangerous Man in Detroit*. Urbana: University of Illinois Press, 1995.

Linder, Marc, and Ingrid Nygaard. *Void Where Prohibited: Rest Breaks and the Right to Urinate on Company Time*. Ithaca, N.Y.: Cornell University Press, 1998.

Lipset, Seymour Martin, and Gary Marks. *It Didn't Happen Here: Why Socialism Failed in the United States*. New York: W. W. Norton, 2000.

Lopez, Stephen. *Reorganizing the Rust Belt: From Business Unionism to Social Movement Unionism*. Berkeley and Los Angeles: University of California Press, 2004.

Lynch, Lisa. "Payoffs to Alternative Training Strategies at Work." In *Working Under Different Rules*, ed. Richard B. Freeman, pp. 63–95. New York: Russell Sage Foundation, 1994.

Lynd, Staughton, and Alice Lynd, eds. *The New Rank And File*. Ithaca, N.Y.: Cornell University Press, 2000.

Manheim, Jarol B. *Death by a Thousand Cuts*. Mahwah, N.J.: Lawrence Erlbaum Associates, 2001.

Mann, Michael. *The Sources of Social Power*, Volume II: *The Rise of Classes and Nation States, 1760–1914*. New York: Cambridge University Press, 1993.

Matles, James J., and James Higgins. *Them and Us: Struggles of a Rank-and-File Union*. Englewood Cliffs, N.J.: Prentice Hall Inc., 1974.

McAlevey, Jane. "It Takes a Community: Building Unions from the Outside in." *New Labor Forum* (spring 2003): 23–32.

Meredith, Robyn. "A Union March on Alabama: UAW Is Facing Uncommon Odds at Mercedes Plant." *The New York Times*, June 29, 1999, p. C27.

Meyerson, Harold. "A Clean Sweep." *The American Prospect*, June 19–July 3, 2000, pp. 30–39.

———. "Street vs. Suite: Why L.A.'s Janitors Will Win Their Strike." *The LA Weekly*, April 7–13, 2000.

Milkman, Ruth. "Immigrant Organizing and the New Labor Movement in Los Angeles." *Critical Sociology* 26, nos. 1–2 (2000): 59–81.

Milkman, Ruth, and Kent Wong. "Organizing Immigrant Workers: Case Studies from Southern California." In *Rekindling the Labor Movement: Labor's Quest for Relevance in the 21st Century*, ed. Lowell Turner, Harry C. Katz, and Richard W. Hurd. Ithaca, N.Y.: Cornell University Press, 2001.

Mills, C. Wright. *The New Men of Power: America's Labor Leaders*. New York: Harcourt, Brace and Company, 1948.

Mishel, Lawrence, Jared Bernstein, and Heather Boushey. *The State of Working America 2002–2003*. Ithaca, N.Y.: Cornell University Press, 2003.

Mishel, Lawrence, Jared Bernstein, and John Schmitt. *The State of Working America 2000–2001*. Ithaca, N.Y.: Cornell University Press, 2000.

Moberg, David. "Organization Man." *The Nation* online, July 16, 2001.

———. "Union Cities: Can Stodgy Old Central Labor Councils Be Transformed into Spearheads of Progressive Local Politics? It's Already Happening." *The American Prospect*, September 11, 2000, pp. 35–38.

———. "Unions Get Religion." *In These Times*, August 21, 2000, p. 25.

Moehring, Eugene. *Resort City in the Sunbelt: Las Vegas 1930–2000*. Reno: University of Nevada Press, 2000.

Moody, Kim. "On Eve of Seattle Trade Protests, Sweeney Endorses Clinton's Agenda." *Labor Notes*, December 1999, p. 1.

———. *An Injury to All: The Decline of American Unionism*. London: Verso, 1988.

Mosle, Sara. "At Hotel Casino, Triumphant Shouts of 'Union!'" *The New York Times*, February 5, 1998, p. A1.

Nazario, Sonia. "Hunger Strike Marks Union's Split." *Los Angeles Times*, August 8, 1995, p. B1.

———. "For this Union, It's War." *Los Angeles Times*, August 19, 1993, p. 1.

Ness, Immanuel. "Organizing Immigrant Communities: UNITE's Workers' Center Strategy." In *Organizing to Win: New Research on Union Strategies,* ed. Kate Bronfenbrenner, Sheldon Friedman, Richard W. Hurd, Rudolph A. Oswald, and Ronald L. Seeber, pp. 87–101. Ithaca, N.Y.: Cornell University Press, 1998.

Ness, Immanuel, and Stuart Eimer, eds. *Central Labor Councils and the Revival of American Unionism.* London: M. E. Sharpe, 2001.

Nissen, Bruce, ed. *Which Direction for Organized Labor?* Detroit, Mich.: Wayne State University Press, 1999.

Ortega, Bob. *In Sam We Trust: The Untold Story of Sam Walton and How Wal-Mart Is Devouring America.* New York: Random House, 1998.

Ozaki, Muneto. *Negotiating Flexibility.* Geneva: International Labour Office, 1999.

Parsons, Talcott, ed. *Max Weber: Social and Economic Organization.* New York: The Free Press, 1947.

Pimentel, Benjamin. "Immigrant Organizers Strengthen U.S. Unions." *The San Francisco Chronicle,* October 8, 1993, p. A3.

Piore, Michael. "Unions: A Reorientation to Survive." In *Labor Economics and Industrial Relations: Markets and Institutions,* ed. Clark Kerr and Paul D. Staudohar, pp. 512–41. Cambridge, Mass.: Harvard University Press, 1994.

Quaglieri, Philip L., ed. *America's Labor Leaders.* Lexington, Mass.: Lexington Books, 1989.

———. "A People's Person." In *America's Labor Leaders,* ed. Philip L. Quaglieri, pp. 197–204. Lexington, Mass.: Lexington Books, 1989.

Pollin, Bob, and Stephanie Luce. *The Living Wage: Building a Fair Economy.* New York: New Press, 1998.

Rachleff, Peter. *Hard Pressed in the Heartland: The Hormel Strike and the Future of the Labor Movement.* Boston: South End Press, 1993.

Rainwater, Lee, and T. M. Smeeding. "Comparing Living Standards Across Nations: Real Incomes at the Top, the Bottom, and the Middle." In *What Has Happened to the Quality of Life in the Advanced Industrialized Nations?* ed. D. B. Papadimitriou and E. N. Wolff. Northampton, Mass.: Edward Elgar Publishing, forthcoming.

Riesman, David. *The Lonely Crowd.* New Haven, Conn., and London: Yale University Press, 1950.

Rosenblum, Jonathan D. *Copper Crucible.* Ithaca, N.Y.: ILR Press, 1995.

Ross, Andrew, ed. *No Sweat.* London: Verso, 1997.

Roth, Kenneth. "Unfair Advantage: Workers' Freedom of Association in the United States under International Human Rights Standards." Testimony of the Executive Director of Human Rights Watch Before the Senate Committee on Health, Education, Labor, and Pensions, June 20, 2002.

Rothenbuhler, E. W. "The Liminal Fight. Mass Strikes as Ritual and Interpretation." In *Durkheimian Sociology,* ed. J. C. Alexander. Cambridge: Cambridge University Press, 1988.

Royster, Deidre. *Race and the Invisible Hand.* Berkeley and Los Angeles: University of California Press, 2002.

Russakoff, Dale. "When Pay Can't Cover Child Care." *International Herald Tribune,* July 7, 2000, p. 12.

Scheirov, Richard. *Pride and Solidarity: A History of the Plumbers and Pipefitters of Columbus, Ohio, 1889–1989.* Ithaca, N.Y.: Cornell University Press, 1993.

Schiffrin, Andrè. *The Business of Books.* London: Verso, 2000.

Schnell, John F., and Cynthia L. Gramm. "The Empirical Relations Between Employers' Striker Replacement Strategies and Strike Duration." *Industrial and Labor Relations Review* 47 (January 1994): 189–206.

Schor, Juliet B. *Do Americans Shop Too Much?* Boston: Beacon Press, 2000.

———. *The Overworked American.* New York: Basic Books, 1991.

Scott, Jerome F., and George Homans. "Reflections on the Wildcat Strikes." *American Sociological Review* 12 (1947): 278–87.

Serrin, William. "Labor Pact at Yale." *The New York Times,* January 24, 1985, p. B4.

———. "An Unorthodox Heads Unionists at Yale." *The New York Times,* February 2, 1985, p. 24.

Sexton, Patricia Cayo. *The War on Labor and the Left: Understanding America's Unique Conservatism.* Boulder, Colo.: Westview Press, 1991.

Sexton, Patricia Cayo, and Brendan Sexton. *Blue Collars and Hard-Hats: The Working Class and the Future of American Politics.* New York: Random House, 1971.

Sherman, Rachel, and Kim Voss. "Organize or Die: Labor's New Tactics and Immigrant Workers." In *Organizing Immigrants: The Challenge for Unions in Contemporary California,* ed. Ruth Milkman, pp. 81–108. Ithaca, N.Y.: Cornell University Press, 2000.

Silverman, Stuart, and Josh Meyer. "Fast Growing Union Hits Obstacles in L.A." *Los Angeles Times,* September 18, 1995, p. A1.

Slaughter, Jane. *Concessions and How to Beat Them.* Detroit, Mich.: Labor Education and Research Project, 1983.

Smeeding, Timothy M. "No Child Left Behind?" *Indicators* 1, no. 3: 6–30.

Smith, Vicki. *Crossing the Great Divide: Worker Risk and Opportunity in the New Economy.* Ithaca, N.Y.: Cornell University Press, 2001.

Sombart, Werner. *Why Is there No Socialism in the United States?* Trans. Patricia M. Hocking and C. T. Husbands. White Plains, N.Y.: International Arts and Science Press, 1976.

Spencer, Charles. *Blue Collar: An Internal Examination of the Workplace.* Chicago, Ill.: Vanguard Books, 1977.

Stepan-Norris, Judith, and Maurice Zeitlin. *Left Out: Reds and America's Industrial Unions.* Cambridge: Cambridge University Press, 2003.

Stevens, Beth. "Blurring the Boundaries: How the Federal Government has Influenced Welfare Benefits in the Private Sector." In *The Politics of Social Policy in the United States,* ed. Margaret Weir, Ann Shola Orloff, and Theda Skocpol, pp. 123–48. Princeton, N.J.: Princeton University Press, 1988.

Strauss, Gary. "The Billionaires Club: New Economy Rockets CEO Pay into the Stratosphere." *USA Today,* April 5, 2000, p. B1.

Tilly, Chris. *Half a Job: Bad and Good Part-Time Jobs in a Changing Labor Market.* Philadelphia, Pa.: Temple University Press, 1996.

Torres, Vicki. "Talking Trash: Strike Supporters Sweep Through Century City." *Los Angeles Times,* June 2, 1990, p. B1.

Tower, Wells. "Sam's Dream; Sam Walton Created a Place where Low-

Wage Workers Aspire to Riches and Lonely Old Men Look for Love at Tuesday Morning Bingo." *The Washington Post Magazine*, October 6, 2002, p. W6.

Trevino, Joseph. "Strike Allies," *The LA Weekly* online, October 20–26, 2000. http://www.laweekly.com/ink/00/48/news-trevino.php

Van Time, Warren R. *The Making of a Labor Bureaucrat*. Amherst: University of Massachusetts Press, 1973.

Van Voorhis, Steve. "Hub Janitors Reach Deal, End Strike." *The Boston Herald*, October 24, 2002, p.1

Vance, Sandra S., and Roy V. Scott. *Wal-Mart: A History of Sam Walton's Retail Phenomenon*. New York: Twayne Publishers, 1994.

Vogel, David. "Why Businessmen Distrust Their State: The Political Consciousness of American Corporate Executives." *British Journal of Political Science* 8 (January 1978). 45–78.

Voss, Kim. *The Making of American Exceptionalism: The Knights of Labor and Class Formation in the Nineteenth Century*. Ithaca, N.Y.: Cornell University Press, 1993.

Voss, Kim, and Rachel Sherman. "Breaking the Iron Law of Oligarchy: Union Revitalization in the American Labor Movement." *American Journal of Sociology* 106 (September 2000): 327–33.

Wacquant, Loic. "The Comparative Structure and Experience of Urban Exclusion: 'Race', Class, and Space in Chicago and Paris." In *Poverty, Inequality, and the Future of Social Policy: Western States in the New World Order*, ed. Katherine McFate, Roger Lawson, and William Julius Wilson, pp. 543–83. New York: Russell Sage Foundation, 1993.

———. *Les Prisons De La Misere*. Paris: Editions Raisons D'Agir, 1999.

———. *Urban Outcasts*. London: Polity, 2003.

Waldinger, Roger, Chris Erickson, Ruth Milkman, Daniel J. B. Mitchell, Abel Valenzuela, Kent Wond, and Maurice Zeitlin. "Helots No More: A Case Study of the Justice for Janitors Campaign in Los Angeles." In *Organizing to Win: New Research on Union Strategies*, ed. Kate Bronfenbrenner, Sheldon Friedman, Richard W. Hurd, Rudolph A. Oswald, and Ronald L. Seeber, pp. 102–20. Ithaca, N.Y.: Cornell University Press, 1998.

Warner, Sam Bass. *Streetcar Suburbs: The Process of Growth in Boston, 1879–1900*. Cambridge, Mass.: Harvard University Press, 1978.

Weir, Margaret. *Politics and Jobs: The Boundaries of Employment Policy in the United States*. Princeton, N.J.: Princeton University Press, 1992.

Western, Bruce. *Between Class and Market*. Princeton, N.J.: Princeton University Press, 1997.

Western, Bruce, and Katherine Beckett. "How Unregulated Is the U.S. Labor Market? The Penal System as a Labor Market Institution." *American Journal of Sociology* 104 (January 1999): 1135–72.

Whyte, William F., Jr. *The Organization Man*. New York: Simon and Schuster, 1956.

Wilson, William Julius. *When Work Disappears*. New York: Alfred A. Knopf, 1996.

Wolff, Edward N. "Recent Trends in Wealth Ownership, 1983–1998." Jerome Levy Economics Institute, April 2000.

———. *Top Heavy*. New York: New Press. 1996.

Zieger, Robert H. *The CIO, 1935–1955*. Chapel Hill: University of North Carolina Press, 1995.

———. "George Meany: Labor's Organization Man." In *Labor Leaders in America*, ed. Melvyn Dubofsky and Warren Van Tine, pp. 324–39. Chicago: University of Illinois Press, 1987.

INDEX

Italicized page numbers refer to diagrams and sidebars.

Compositor: BookMatters, Berkeley
Indexer: Sharon Sweeney
Text: 10/15 Janson
Display: Janson
Printer and Binder: Sheridan Books, Inc.